PIECES:

Constructing the Identity Puzzle
A Christian Perspective

Candace Q. Powell

ISBN 978-1-0980-9660-1 (paperback)
ISBN 978-1-0980-9661-8 (digital)

Christian Faith Publishing, Inc.
832 Park Avenue
Meadville, PA 16335
www.christianfaithpublishing.com

Printed in the United States of America

Contents

Introduction

Have you ever focused on assembling a puzzle and got to a piece that wasn't cut perfectly and so it just wouldn't fit? You literally had to force it into place, and the entire piece ripped, a corner ripped, or the piece buckled the whole puzzle. Although small, each intricate puzzle piece creates the entire puzzle. You cannot leave one piece out, even if it isn't cut perfectly because it will disrupt the intended picture.

That's pretty much how I have felt my whole life. I was that jagged edge of the puzzle piece that wasn't quite cut right. You see, it wasn't that something was wrong with me; it was just that I felt different, unique, and a little odd. I knew that I had been formed with some jagged edges of my own. We all have imperfections but trying to force-fit into a place where you don't belong will cause you to rip; it will buckle your entire life.

I spent more than two decades focused on living in a forced identity that wasn't quite my own. It wasn't because I was not driven, disciplined, or successful. It was because I didn't know my purpose in life. It was so easy to hide behind my degrees, my accomplishments, work experience, family, and marriage. Although I had familial support, most supported the identity that I lived within and not who I was meant to be. It was not because people were not there for me; certainly many were. It was more that I was not living in a way where I welcomed "me" to be present without the restrictions that I, and others, had placed on my life. No one could support something that they really didn't know existed; so I could not blame anyone else. However, I didn't know how to support "me" either. Consequently, I was left feeling out of place most of my life.

Uncovering your identity and life purpose means that you are obligated to permit "you" to be present. This process is not always easy or straightforward. It takes patience and change, both of which do not occur overnight. Often, it is a painful experience to examine oneself and to be objective. Some questions you must ask yourself:

What does it mean to allow "me" to be present? Am I living as my truest self? How do I support being the *real* me? How do I grow in confidence to allow "me" to be present without fear if I'm lacking confidence? Have I addressed any issues with self-esteem, rejection, emotional pain, damage, or hurt? Have I examined the lies that I have convinced myself are real and valid? Am I deeply or unconsciously concerned with the thoughts and opinions of others, or am I obsessed with negative opinions about myself?

What is motivating me to find who I really am? Is it to prove people wrong about me, get back at someone, or to prove something to myself? Or am I motivated by discovering the liberty, inner peace, and happiness that follows living in my purpose? Do I really want to do this?

Am I comfortable going on this journey without the support that I think I need or deserve? Am I comfortable working on myself even if I feel that I am all alone? Do I really want to go on the journey of finding my purpose and discovering my authentic identity? Am I ready to do the work that it will require? Am I ready to act or just read another book on how to help myself? Am I ready to make this process my own or will I just read it as a story of someone else?

Stolen Dream

You Stole from me
I had a dream that was all mine,
Fresh, young, and still undefined.
I knew that hard work was the way to get there,
And I did just that… I worked hard, sacrificed to the point where I
    almost cracked,
But I didn't plan for you to stand
in my way
Or to redefine my dream for me, pressure me, that there was another
    way.
You see, I wanted to live my life the way I planned, not be forced by
    your hand,
to walk in your dried footsteps or repeat your failed cries for help.
You stole from me.
You told me my goals were not good enough,
That I was inadequate and my hopes just frivolous stuff.
I tried a new direction, and even then, you picked that apart at your
    own discretion.
You inhaled my dreams like secondhand smoke, charred in burned
    throats, swallowing the vapors before I had the chance to
    choke…on my own dreams.
You see, you stole from me.
You told me what to do and how to do it and you left no room for
    mistakes,
Even when perfection was my name, you took credit for that and
    crushed my efforts at the gates.

Yeah, you stole from me.

I knew what I wanted to do, what my purpose was.

I could smell the hope of my dream but never taste it because

You took the life and soul of my inspiration, you used it to glorify
yourself and as a decoration.

You dismissed my pain and left me broken,

You paraded my distress as your own personal token.

You made my dream your own, my success your own, my glory your
own, my accolades your own.

You see, you stole from me.

You made me believe that my dream was not worth having,

Like I was wasting my time, because in your life, things were not
happening.

You see, you stole from me.

You used your life as an excuse for mine,

Like because you failed, I would do the same in time.

But you stole from me.

You see, my dreams could have come true, if you hadn't quenched
my fire with your dirty water of negativity, instability, and lack
of upward mobility.

But again, you stole from me.

My dream would have come to pass, if only you would have let it last,
at least an hour, a minute, a second.

At least long of enough for me to determine a path not polluted with
your poisonous vermin.

You see, my dream could have come true,

Only if I listened to myself instead of you.

You stole from me.

Chapter 1

Identity Theft

Worst Class of Criminals

Identity thieves are roughly the worst class of criminals because they operate secretly, skillfully, and typically without immediate detection. In 2019 alone, "14.4 million consumers became victims of identity fraud—that's about 1 in 15 people."[1] Daily, there are numerous victims who are unaware that their identity has been compromised until it is too late. We aim to protect our IDs, social security cards, birth certificates, passports, and all official documents because we understand the value that these documents hold. They not only help to ensure that we are who we say we are, but proper identification comes with privileges, such as making large purchases, international air travel, and gaining access to funds. Accurate identification permits a person to function with autonomy and freedom in our modern world.

What would happen if you needed to withdraw a large sum of money from your bank account but didn't have proper identification? Of course, you would get denied access to your funds. Even though the funds belong to you, without proper identification, they

---

[1] Jennifer Bellamare, "What Are the Odds of Getting Your Identity Stolen?" *Identity Force* (Jan. 2, 2018, updated July 2, 2020; accessible at https://www.identityforce.com/blog/identity-theft-odds-identity-theft-statistics, retrieved July 27, 2020).

cannot be released to you, for your own safety and protection. This is the same risk that we take spiritually and naturally when we do not understand our own identity. We block our own access from spiritual gifts, purpose, and our natural calling when we cannot grasp who we are. We must ask ourselves the important question "Who am I really?"

Are You at Risk?

Typically, in your youth, you have dreams of becoming something "big;" your views are limitless, and you feel like you could reach the stars. You may want to become a firefighter, a doctor, a police officer, a scientist, or, like my oldest son when he was three, a Power Ranger. There are so many infinite possibilities when you are a child. When you are young, your dreams are undefined because your identity is unrefined. This is not because God does not know who you are or what He wants for you; it is because you are not mature enough to understand His plan or why He made you in your own uniqueness.

As a youngster, you are in the process of learning, growing, and developing into the person you are meant to become. Naturally, you notice some strengths and some weaknesses, and you learn to make decisions on your own. Generally, you are told to work hard, to set appropriate goals, to make sacrifices to reach your goals, and if you work just hard enough, things will work out for you. Yet, what happens when you follow these seemingly wise instructions and you wind up in a place that doesn't fit who you are? Or after a culmination of all your efforts you do not feel as though you have landed in a place that feels worthwhile?

How does this happen? How do you even recognize that you are going in an erroneous direction? If not in error, how do you know that the "right" direction that you seem to be taking will lead you to the landing point that you desire?

I could not comprehend or fathom how I once knew what I wanted to do and which direction I felt was natural for me, but suddenly, nothing made sense anymore. It was as if my dream was stolen from me. Has anyone ever taken something from you? Have you ever felt robbed of something? Have you ever felt the pain of knowing that you once owned something of value and someone else came, without consideration, and stole your valuable item away? You are left feeling helpless and powerless. This is what happens during identity theft, pun intended. You literally lose your value because you are robbed of what belongs to you.

Not knowing your true identity means that you cannot adequately protect yourself, and thus, your lack of clarity opens you up for robbery. When you don't know who you are, the enemy, along with others, can and will steal from you. In John 10:10, it says that "the thief cometh not, but for to steal, and to kill, and to destroy: I am come that they might have life, and that they might have it more abundantly" (KJV). You may ask yourself, what is the enemy or anyone else going to steal? It's simple: your dreams, your purpose, your value, your gifts, and whatever uniqueness you have to offer. Not to mention your peace, your joy, your laughter, and the very essence of why you exist. What is the point of living if you are not living in purpose and on purpose? Your purpose should be completely encompassed in the God-identity that He has given each individual, including you.

Restricted

If you lack understanding concerning your identity, others can define you and lock you into a box that restricts who you were meant to be. What's worse, you will consistently come into agreement with those limitations and further restrict yourself. When you do not know who you are meant to be, you will open yourself up to bad advice and perverted wisdom. You may even allow people to counsel you from in impure place. Their wisdom may come from a place of pain or it may be grounded in the mistakes that they made themselves.

Listening or adhering to impure wisdom can limit what is possible for you. Someone else's failures or mistakes should not determine your path or direction. People will attempt to get you to avoid going down a certain path, simply because they were unsuccessful going a similar route. This is not usually the best type of counsel because it is guided from a place of fear instead of a perspective of opportunity and godly potential. If God is leading you down a way that seems unprecedented, obey the voice of God. He may have created you to be a pioneer.

I'm in no way saying that experience does not provide wisdom, because it certainly can, but it is best to receive wisdom from people who have clarity in their lives and no ulterior motives. God has not intended for us to live foolishly or to make unnecessary mistakes, but someone else's mistakes does not equate to wisdom or perspective for your entire life. For this reason, distinguishing between your identity and the identity of others is essential to making sound life decisions. Remember, if someone is attempting to use your thumbprint to access your phone, they will be **restricted**. Some things are meant for you to unlock only through a process that God has designed for you.

Friendly Fire

As you embark on the journey of identity exploration, one critical truth that you must consider is that all support is not supportive. Taking advice from friends and family can prove to be detrimental if their guidance is not spirit-led. Family members may be supportive, but they may be supporting the identity that you live within and not who you really are or the person that you will become.

It is also common for friends and family to not give your dreams a chance or to only support you in an area where they already perceive you to be successful. Countless times, they are looking through a lens of themselves. Some may be trying to live vicariously through you, some may be jealous of you, and some may be limited in their view of your potential because they too, do not know themselves.

Respect and love your family and friends but do not allow them to create your identity for you. Allow God to work in you the things that He has intrinsically designed for you and your purpose. You will be at your greatest peace when you are walking in an identity that was tailor-made for you. If you live for other people, you will sacrifice the greatest gifts that are in you, and you will be left feeling void and shallow. Follow the process that God has you on and learn to listen carefully for His instructions while respecting and honoring those around you.

This doesn't mean that you must agree with what your friends or family believe about you, but because intimate relationships are a part of our lives, choose carefully how and when to reveal if God is leading you in a different direction than what they may have expected. It may be necessary to separate from your family for a season to allow God to work on you, only to be reunited with them later. If this happens, just remember that it is only a temporary situation and trust God's process to define you, lead you, and guide you to His truth and understanding.

In the book of Exodus, chapters twelve and thirteen, the Lord instructed Moses to gather the people of Israel for the Passover as he prepared them to leave Egypt. The Lord commanded that when it was time to eat the Passover, all the people were required to be fully clothed, with their shoes on their feet, a walking stick in their hand, and prepared for travel. They were dressed for war (Exodus 12:11 ESV). Of course, Pharaoh initially denied the people of Israel the right to depart Egypt, but eventually He forced them to leave.

When they left, God did not allow them to travel the shortest route through the land of the Philistines because they would have had to go to war with them. Even though the people of Israel would not necessarily want to go to war with the Philistines, the Philistines would assume that they were coming for a war simply because of how they were fully dressed in their war clothes and because they were carrying all the goods from which they spoiled from the Egyptians. God did not want the pressures, fears, and burdens of a war to lead their minds back to Egypt where they were in bondage.

The significance of this particular point is to realize that when you are going through your identity-discovery process, you may encounter many battles and some wars. Not only does God want you to go through this process fully, He does not want you to take any shortcuts, even if it appears to be beneficial. The shortest route is not always best. Even more significantly, as you begin to discover who you are in God, you may go through a process of deliverance and freedom. Some people may get intimidated by you because once you begin to discover who you are, you will change and begin to fight for the right to be you. This means that you will be clothed in war clothes. In other words, you may become stronger, defensive, and more in tune with your truest self.

Once you leave the bondage of Egypt and living in your old identity, you'll be so happy to be free and to be yourself, that your enemy, friends, and family may not be able to recognize you. Sometimes, they won't know if you have changed for the better or for the worse and may feel threatened by your changes. During this process, you may encounter friendly fire.

Friendly fire is defined as "weapon fire coming from one's own side that causes accidental injury or death to one's own forces."[2] Others around you may be unsettled by your changes and attack you for them. Do not allow friendly fire to overwhelm you, permanently injure you, or veer you off course. Remain planted in the process and on the path in which God is leading you. Protect your authentic identity and resist the urge to please the opinions of others as you begin to transform.

Robbed of Grace

I grew up in an environment that was strict and that welcomed little room for grace. Even the smallest mistake was scolded or responded to as a catastrophe. For me, this grew into a spirit of perfectionism. Perfectionism is an identity thief because it robs you of the opportunity to have grace for your mistakes and to give yourself room to grow. Although we should all strive for excellence, perfectionism can cause you to be overly hard on yourself and contributes to negative thinking. You will not be able to discover your identity with negative thought patterns and by habitually beating yourself up, even over small errors.

It is important to know the areas in your life where there is room for improvement, but it's equally important to not focus only

---

[2] *Oxford Dictionary*, s. v. "friendly fire" (accessed July 27, 2020, from https://www.lexico.com/definition/friendly_fire).

on negative aspects, missteps, or occasional blunders. This is mentally unhealthy and spiritually detrimental. It is critical to recognize ways in which to healthily release your pain and your mistakes and to have positive outlets to do so. More importantly, it is crucial to have individuals within your life who will support you when you are feeling a great deal of pain. This is because pain has a way of blocking your clarity, dulling your passion, and masking your identity.

Life Support

Having access to the right people is such a crucial component of identity discovery because the wrong people can confuse, discourage, or disengage you from your purpose. Contrarily, the right people can affirm, support, challenge, and help you to grow.

In my life, there were times that I tried to communicate my level of pain and distress, but because I did not have the appropriate support system, I felt as if my pain was belittled and ignored. It seemed that my pain was less important than what I was told I needed to accomplish. It was as if I was supposed to push through the pain instead of learning how to deal with the core issues that I was facing. Many well-intentioned people tried to help me, but I didn't always have the "right" people around me.

When others dismissed my true feelings, I was left feeling numb and depressed. This robbed me of my ability to have healthy emotions. I struggled to understand how to appropriately respond to others, and for a while, I even shut off my emotions altogether. It was very easy for me to emotionally detach if I needed to because of the amount of trauma I experienced. At this point in my life, I was not living. I was surviving on life-support. If it wasn't for God allowing me to go through the motions of life, I may have simply given up. I did not know how to breathe or get through what I was experiencing on my own. I needed help!

Stripping the Layers

Unhealthy emotions prevent you from building lasting relationships. They skew your worldview, affect your level of intimacy with others, and limit what you think is possible for you. It reinforces the fears and restrictions you have already placed on yourself. Unhealthy emotions are another identity thief because they rob you of the possibility of digging deeper. They cause you to only look at your problems from a surface level and to hide behind your flaws. Real identity discovery requires you to truly examine your weaknesses and work on strengthening them.

My best friend and husband always says, "It is easier to strengthen your strengths but much harder to strengthen your weaknesses." What is central to discovering who you are is knowing yourself better. Although others can give you insight, it is essential that you reach deeper into God, press into the layered components of yourself, to learn what He's saying or has already spoken about you. If you listen to God, you'll understand who you are in Him; especially because you were created in His image.

If you are in a place where you do not have the "right" type of support that you need, it is okay. Although it makes your discovery process more difficult, each person goes through periods of feeling alone or without support. What's critical in these seasons is your ability to trust God and allow Him to be your greatest supporter and advocate. Eventually, He will send the "right" relationships to you. Be patient and continue your journey, even if you feel alone. Know that He is always with you, even if no one else is.

Depression

Depression is another powerful identity thief. Depression is a dark force that seeks to destroy you without your permission and sometimes without your knowledge or compliance. It drowns your energy, suffocates your passion and disrupts your cognitive ability to see and respond with clarity. Depression promotes self-pity, inaction, and fear. It exhausts you of physical energy, stamina, and motivation. If you are experiencing depression, it will be very difficult for you to hear God concerning your purpose and your identity. You will spend more time feeling sorry for yourself, complaining about what's not fair, and sulking, than you will spend seeking God for your purpose. Depression robs you of the vigor and energy you need to actively seek God. It kills your momentum, your drive, and your strength to tap into the power of God.

The Bible describes depression as the "spirit of heaviness" in Isaiah 61:3 (KJV). He also provided a remedy for heaviness which is described as the "garment of praise." When you are feeling heavy, discouraged, and hopeless, praising God is a tested method for reversing your slump. I believe that the significance of praise being described as a garment is to show that a garment is something you wear or put on to clothe yourself. You typically would not go outside without being clothed, even if you did not feel like getting dressed when you woke up. This is important because typically when you are feeling depressed and trapped in despair, you do not feel like doing anything at all.

Putting on a garment of praise means that you must wear "praise," whether you feel like it or not. It's like wearing a smile. You may not feel like smiling but smiling more often and more consistently can help you to feel better about yourself. Simply putting on praise or praising God when you don't feel good about yourself can overturn your heaviness. This process will plant you in God's righteousness, and He will ultimately be glorified.

Armed Robbery

As a child, I felt robbed because around the age of eight, I wanted to be an author. Simple, you might think. However, I was told that writing would make a good hobby but that I would have to get a "real" job. I was immediately crushed and harbored feelings of inadequacy.

Later in life as a teen, I was fascinated with fashion and design. I would spend hours designing clothing, textiles, and watching runway shows. I decided in high school that I wanted to go to college for fashion design. Again, I was told that fashion design wasn't a "real" career or that it wasn't as promising as a "real" job. My mother, well-intentioned, was doing her best to raise me without any paternal support. She only wanted the best for me and pushed me in the direction that she believed would result in the best outcome for my life. She was doing what she thought was best for me without really *knowing* "me." I've seen the sad reality of comments and guidance such as this, not only in my life but in the lives of others.

Consequently, I settled for going to college for business because I thought that in business, I could find a "real" job. I watched as many others went to college for things in which they were genuinely interested, while I felt defeated and lost. I didn't realize at that time that I was fighting against a word curse for my own creativity. I was told to do something more *serious* because my goals weren't perceived as good enough.

My mother didn't intend any harm and later encouraged me to write and to use my creativity, but at that time, she didn't realize what she had said to me. I learned that parents, no matter how well-intentioned, may think they know what's best for you but often may not even know who "you" are.

Sometimes, your parents were not allowed to be who *they* really were. They then parent you from a place of pain or from a place of their own personal failures. They only want to protect you from failure or going in the wrong direction. They want to ensure your success. How many times do you hear of the person who is majoring in art, only to hear everyone else discourage them because everyone knows they won't get a *real job*? I do not blame my mother because she did an amazing job raising me, but I often felt inadequate and robbed of being myself because I was not allowed to go in the direction that was natural for me. Not only was I left feeling inadequate, I was left feeling inferior and out of place.

I recently read a post on Facebook about a young lady who is an artist and who decided to go to college as an art major. She explained how many people encouraged her to pursue a major that was "more promising" or a major that would pay her "real" money. She realized early on who she was and that she needed to learn how to further perfect her craft. Just because someone else cannot see the value in her majoring in art does not mean that she will be unable to become a successful artist or that she isn't one already. She has found who she is and is comfortable pursing her art!

What's really disturbing about the comments of her critics is that what they are really saying is that they don't believe in her. They truly do not believe that she will be able to earn a sizeable income from her artwork or they believe that her degree isn't worth it. Now, does this mean that every art major will become a successful artist? Absolutely not! However, in all fairness, she believes that she is called to art in a way that speaks to her true identity. Besides, any degree is only as valuable as you make it. No one can determine your *true* worth like your Creator.

Honestly, there are people with degrees in all sorts of "more promising" career paths, and many of those people do not have jobs, careers, or a substantial income. In fact, many of those same people have student loan debt, a job that they hate, and spend tons of money on valueless things trying to escape life and find their true "intrinsic value." I certainly wish that I had the revelation of this this young lady when I was her age. I may have pursued my art earlier in life and I probably would have saved myself time and money. My main issue was that I didn't understand how to effectively activate my passions in the right direction. I did not know who I was, and I only looked at the world through the lens of how others said it worked. *BIG MISTAKE!*

If this has happened to you, do not give up hope because if you seek God, you will get back on the path that He wants for you. You may feel that you have wasted time and resources in the wrong areas, but God has a way of teaching you through your mistakes and redeeming your lost time and efforts. Although at the time I did not see how majoring in business would become a part of God's master plan, it turns out that it would still be a part of my identity after all. God has a way of intricately assembling the pieces of your life puzzle together in ways you may never understand. It's important to recognize that mistakes are just as important as your successes. Each shapes your life for the better.

As a parent myself, I sometimes find it difficult to "know" my children, and I often challenge myself to "see" them and not partially "see" what I want for them. I take the time to listen to them and to truly *hear* them even when providing discipline and direction. I also pray for them and over their lives so that they will be aligned with who God wants them to be. I do not want to simply raise good citizens, but I want to steward the call of future prophetic, Kingdom leaders in the body of Christ. They were His prophetic heritage and His promise before they ever became my children.

The most dangerous element of not knowing your identity is that you remain open to confusion from Satan. We have all heard and read in the Bible that it is his purpose to kill, steal, and destroy. Yet we often do not actively think about his efforts to steal our identity. We may think about it passively, but Satan works aggressively and tirelessly to ensure that we never become what God wants us to become. He not only attempts to steal our identity, he encourages us to spend time and to put resources into the wrong areas. He knows that the fewer resources we have and the more energy we put into the wrong areas, the less the time and resources we will have to devote to the "right" areas. He actively works to steal our identity, our resources, and our time. Ultimately, this destroys our zeal, youth, passion, and energy sources. God calls the young because they are strong. But when you are robbed of your youth and strength by the enemy, it makes it more challenging, but not impossible, to pursue your godly purpose.

Satan puts as many roadblocks in our way as possible to get us to abandon the search for identifying who we really are. Finding your identity requires a relationship with God because we are made in God's image. Knowing the Father helps us to know ourselves better. However, when you are lacking clarity in identity, Satan comes with mixed messages about what you should be doing. He will use negative self-talk, negative thoughts, and even other people to speak death to your purpose. He will use any and everything he can to deter you from the path that God wants. You must learn how to tune out those negative thoughts and command your thoughts by setting them on the things of God. You must carefully learn how to hear and listen to the voice of God and rebuke the words of the enemy.

Passion vs. Purpose

What clearly sets apart the young lady who knows that her purpose involves her art is that she understands that her art is not simply a passion or a hobby. One thing that frustrated me and something that I would put in the category of bad advice, is that I would hear people say all of the time, pursue your passion and the money will come later. I never understood this mindset because truthfully, it does not always work out that way for everyone.

Some people have pursued passion, but passion does not necessarily equate to purpose. Frequently, our passions come from our life experiences, and if our experiences have been limited, then our passions will be limited too. Purpose is more than just passion. It's a part of your identity, your calling, and what you are designed to do. Thus, knowing your identity is essential to living your best purposeful life.

For example, I became a mother very young and was challenged in ways that I could have never imagined. Naturally, I was passionate about helping other young mothers because I had been one myself. However, just because I experienced something and could relate to it did not mean that working to help young mothers was my "calling" in life. It was my experience and I was very passionate about it but that did not necessarily equate to my calling.

Please don't get into the habit of making your passion your purpose. Although it is possible that some or all of your passions may lead to your purpose, or may already be aligned with your purpose, do not assume that this process is automatic. Intentionally identify whether your passions have originated solely from life experiences or if they are genuinely connected to your identity because of God's plans.

Often people who do not know who they are will pursue purpose based on their experience and not on their identity. I cannot tell you how many people have spent years pursing passions that were either hobbies or something that they enjoyed but wasn't their life's purpose. Subsequently, they may not have had "the money come later" as many people told them would happen. There are always exceptions to this, and this is not a hard-and-fast rule; carefully examine your circumstances on an individual basis.

In my case, I did not have a clear understanding of my identity or my purpose, and as a result of this, I pursued a career at an income level that allowed me to take care of myself. This was practical but not fulfilling. At the end of the day, I had to eat, pay bills, and live. So I did what worked for me. Practicality is not always the best solution for some, but it could be. This is why each person must assess what God desires for them as an individual and seek His sound wisdom. Never rely on the fears and limitations of others.

Being Practical

There is no one-size-fits-all solution to life, so we need to exercise a bit of common sense. Each person should do what's practical for their life situation until they gain an understanding of what God has designed for them. It was my preference to pursue a career at a favorable income level until I could discover what I was meant to do. This process allowed me to fail more quickly, learn from my mistakes, and pivot myself in a more precise direction.

I have seen people simply delay doing anything at all because they do not know what to do. People can become so afraid of wasting time and money that they do nothing. Usually doing nothing will produce nothing, and living a life of simply waiting does not equate to discovery. You must actively pursue something to learn more about yourself. Sometimes, it is only on the road of pursuit, even if it's something that will not become be your end goal, that you encounter your *true* purpose.

Stop and Reflect

These reflection sections are times for you to evaluate what you have just read and participate in a simple exercise. Try not to skip; although you will tell yourself that you will come back to it, you likely will not. Do not create bad habits. Instead, do the work and notice the changes. Simply get out your journal or a pad of paper and have it ready while you read.

Now that you have a general understanding of identity theft, you must make the active decision to examine yourself.

1. Write down all of the areas of your life in which you believe your identity was stolen.
2. Write down why you believe you allowed yourself to become a victim. Was it something you could control or not?
3. Now that you are aware that you may have been a victim, how long will you remain a victim?
4. If it was something that you could not control, have you been able to forgive what happened to you?
5. What are some things you can do to take control to ensure that you never become a victim again? If you can, jot down at least three things.
6. How do you think you can get your identity back?

Chapter 2

Identity Crisis

Suppressed Identity Unleashes Relationship Disasters

There is nothing more disastrous and dangerous than entering relationships prior to authentic identity revelation. Establishing relationships prematurely can compromise the quality of those same relationships, affect their lifespan, and dull your pursuit for authentic identity discovery and purposeful living. Both romantic and platonic relationships affect your identity-discovery process because the nature of all relationships demand your time, energy, and "the real you" to be present in complete authenticity.

Note I will mainly focus on romantic relationships in this chapter. Romantic relationships can be more hazardous to your identity-discovery process because they are easy to hide behind. It is convenient to lose yourself "in love" with a person, their character, and their identity. Romance has a way of penetrating your genuine emotional state and creating a facade filled with conflicting sentiments.

Romance also provides a way for you to bury the facts and escape from the reality of your present situation and or circumstances. It allows you to suppress your true identity for the sake of love. So you may make exceptions in places or for a person that you normally would not. Despite the potential positive benefits of all relationships, you must work deliberately to examine how those very relationships may be impacting your ability to determine who you are meant to be.

Signs that a relationship is having a positive impact on you will indicate a challenge for you to grow, to improve, and to progress toward your purpose. It does not mean that you will always be in perfect harmony or agreement, but these relationships will fuel your identity process. They will repudiate stagnation and regression. These relationships will help you to confront your fears, weaknesses, and dysfunctional behavior. On the other hand, relationships that support your false identity and your bad habits and behaviors, or even encourage them, are detrimental to uncovering the real you. They affect and destroy your distinctive character.

It is important to carefully enter relationships with foresight, focusing on the future, and with your gaze set on both short- and long-term goals. If you inspect your relationships with unbiased scrutiny, and you determine that the people you currently engage with should not be a part of your present or your future within the next five years, then it is time to make some active decisions to change. Of course, this is easier said than done. Nevertheless, you must take each day and consciously choose to be around the people who are good for you and depart those who are not.

Learning Everything About You

Growing up, I was not the kind of girl who dreamed I would ever get married. I was definitely a "girly-girl" but I grew up with a single mother and I did not have any examples in my home life that characterized a wife. I didn't really think about marriage as a possibility. Because I also struggled with my self-esteem, I absolutely did not know if anyone would ever want to marry me. Can someone shout "identity crisis"?

I reasonably thought that I would be a single, successful, unwed woman without any children. Wow! Looking back, I had such a narrow view of what life could offer and how I limited what God could have for me. Although my perceptions were formulated around the women that I had relationships with during that time, all the successful women that I knew were unmarried and without children. When I examined more carefully I how defined success, I realized that I defined their success by their careers, the money that they earned, and their perceived status.

These women were Christians and, in my mind, they were living the dream. My initial perspective of success was erroneous because my definition lacked identity in God. I simply thought that declaring oneself as a Christian was enough. Even though I looked up to them as Christian women, being a Christian does not automatically equate to living in purpose. Instead of focusing mainly on abstaining from sinful living, we must also focus on what we are called to live for. Purpose is about learning what you were born to do and why God chose you to do it.

I did not immediately recognize that many of those women actually desired to be married, and some did marry later on. The reason this is significant is because I adopted erroneous foundational views about possible expectations in my life. This is because my ideas about my identity were indistinguishable from the life that I was living during that time. I did not have deep foresight into the future, and I based my expectations around what I could see and perceive and not in faith or purpose in God.

I am not suggesting in any way that marriage is for everyone or that everyone should even want to be married. However, many of us hold close foundational views about our life, what we expect, and where we are going to end up. These views are commonly based on false identity perceptions that we have created, vague identity formulation, or lack of complete identity clarification in general. I am simply challenging you to examine those foundational views that you have held on to prior to learning who you really are.

If you are still in the discovery process, it's difficult to say where you will end up or what is or is not for you when you do not know *everything* about "you"! Reexamination and seeking God is essential. I did not even think marriage was a possibility until my relationship surfaced. I was completely caught off guard and unprepared for its journey. Although my relationship blossomed and became beautiful, my lack of identity clarification brought about painful experiences, mistakes, and circumstances that completely unsettled me and almost took my life. Again, I cannot stress enough that reexamination and seeking God is essential!

Major Changes = Identity Disruptions

When you decide to embark on the journey of a serious relationship, have a baby, get married, buy a house, or make any major decision, people will offer a mass of unsolicited advice and suggestions. A wise woman once told me to place all advice on a shelf, and if I ever needed it, I could dust it off and apply it. Otherwise, I could allow all of that unsolicited advice to collect dust. This instruction was helpful to me because when you are unclear about making certain decisions, you will either listen to everything and everyone, or you will reject everything and everyone. Neither is wise. It takes time to create a balance that fits what works for your individual situation.

When I met my husband, we did not have a traditional court-ship, which is a story all in and of itself. Nevertheless, we were married by the time I was twenty and he was twenty-four. We were awfully young, and we had a daughter a few weeks after we were married. Suddenly my entire life seemed to stall. I was plunged headfirst into the role of a mother and wife without really knowing my identity. Of course, I thought that I had it all figured out and it seemed easy… at first.

It was not long that my marriage began to experience some serious trouble. Most of it was because I did not understand who I was. I looked at my life and thought, this is not me. It was not that I did not have clear goals, ambition, or that I did not know my likes or dislikes. It was more! I was lacking purpose. I was living the life of a wife and mother, and that was it. I felt so defeated and confused. "Whose life is this?" I often asked myself.

When you first get married, people tell you that relationships are all about compromise and communication. Compromise? I thought, okay, that's easy…a little give and take. Communication? We "talk" all of the time about everything. In fact, there is nothing that we cannot discuss. Little did I know that compromise really meant change, and communication was more than just talking about anything and everything. We were two that needed to become one. Frankly, what "two becoming one" describes is two jagged puzzles pieces coming together. It's the process of shaving individual pieces off yourself so that you can better fit with someone else. However, you cannot lose "yourself" in this process.

Now, I know that everyone has heard that it takes two whole people coming together to make a complete marriage. You do not want two broken people coming together attempting to make one whole. Well, the truth is, that is true and great in theory, but it was not my experience and it is not the experience of most people that I know. The main reason this usually becomes a fantasy is because you do not really know how whole or how broken you really are until you must live, grow, and change with another person. Intimate, committed relationships have a way of uncovering hidden, deeply rooted glitches that often remain hidden until the relationship surfaces and matures.

Prior to getting married, I did not feel broken or lost or confused. In fact, I felt great! I did not really know what to expect but I thought it was going to be awesome. I could finally spend all the time in the world with my best friend and the person I loved. Although I have a great marriage today, I was due for a serious wake-up, call and it would come sooner than I expected.

Two Become One = Change

Just like any puzzle, a marriage is not whole when all of the pieces required to make it complete don't properly align or fit together. When two people begin the journey to becoming one, they must be willing to change pieces of themselves for the benefit of the other person. This doesn't mean that you forgo your entire identity, but it means that you should be willing to compromise in order to improve your relationship. Simply put, you must "grow up."

In today's fragile-relationship society, many people are too selfish for this process. They say things such as "you should love me and accept me the way that I am" or "if you really love me, you shouldn't expect me to change." Although a person should love and accept your for being you, the truth is, all of us must change to become the best version of ourselves and to mirror Christ. We all naturally change as we grow and mature into the man or woman we are meant to be. Spouses will often say when they are hurt, "You are not the person that I married!" Truthfully, no one should be exactly the same after you have been married for some time. Each person has a right to grow and to mature.

Frequently, this means that you will notice changes in your partner's actions, personality, and demeanor. These changes may be expected or unexpected and, more importantly, may not be changes that you will always like. Many spouses can be immature; they may not understand the changes that their spouses experience, and may not adapt to those postmarital changes appropriately. It's important to remember that you will not get very far in any marriage without *real* change.

Allow me to explain further with a practical example. When we were first married, my husband had a job that would require him to come home late sometimes. It was not an everyday occurrence, but it sometimes happened. If he was going to be late, I would *naturally* expect him to call me. Well, this soon became an area of contention because he would often forget to call or think it was not important to call. Why? Prior to us being married, he did not have to be accountable to anyone other than himself. He was used to doing things a certain way because it was the way he always did them. If he was late, he did not have someone that he had to check in with. Consequently, within our relationship, checking in with me did not seem important enough for him to remember. He also felt like since he was an adult and not a child, it really was not that big of a deal.

Naturally, I decided that all we needed to do was "talk" about this and the problem would be solved. I explained to him that if he did not check in, I might get worried and think something happened to him. I assumed that everyone called when they were late, and since it was a big deal to me, he should just call. Problem solved, right? Not exactly! We allowed this tiny area of contention to become a full-blown argument. Soon, he accused me of being too worrisome, emotional, and overreacting. I accused him of being insensitive, unresponsive to my needs, and forgetful. It was one thing for me to say that he was insensitive and unresponsive to my needs, but saying he was forgetful made him feel that I was saying he was incompetent. You can probably see where this is going.

This situation grew worse when he decided to make a few stops or visit friends after work without telling me. To be clear, I did not mind him coming home late from work, wanting to spend time with his friends, or taking time for himself, but I did expect to at least know about it. Quickly, we realized that one of us was going to have to change. We needed a compromise. Also we needed to work on our communication skills because what *I really wanted him to hear was that I valued him, I cared about his safety, and I wanted to be respected.* What he really wanted me to hear was that nothing was likely to happen to him, that I should not assume the worst would happen, that sometimes he was stressed and needed a break, and most of all, he was **not** incompetent.

Many people who are planners like me would assume that it's common sense to call if you're going to be late. Trust me, this is what I thought. However, I had not considered that some people do not think this way or were not raised this way. I came into the relationship with my own perceived values of what was "normal" or "common sense," and my husband did as well.

I used this example because it's quite funny now, but it's also easily relatable. How many people have simply wanted a call when someone was running late? Almost everyone. But who was going to make the change in this situation? Was I going to change and say, "It's okay if you do not call; I won't worry; I'll always trust that you're okay?" Or was he going to change and make the effort to call if he was late? Well, the truth is, we **both** changed. He did begin to call when he was late, but occasionally he would forget, and sometimes even until this day, he still **does** forget. I changed because I had to learn to expect the call, but if I did not get it, I would not freak out and worry every time. I would not nag him when he did return, I would encourage him to call next time, and immediately forgive him. We must realize that as humans, we often forget the **little** things.

What would have happened if only I changed, if only he changed, or if neither of us changed? This *little* miscommunication of needs and wants could have turned into a major marriage catastrophe. I've learned that it's not the big things that rip you apart as much as it is the subtle annoyances that drive you crazy every day. Sometimes it's easier to forgive a large blunder than to look over those little, everyday irritations that drive apart people in relationships. I call them the "little foxes." It's these little things that grow and fester into major marital contentions. It doesn't appear this way at first, but if you often look back at your relationships, you will find that the smallest irritations often had a greater effect on your daily life than anything else. It's like having a paper cut on the same finger every time. It's just painful and annoying.

This small example shows that in marriage, as you begin to mature, you will definitely need to make changes that will benefit the "two of you becoming one." Changing into the best version of you requires maturity, and maturity is a large part of learning identity.

Do Not Lose Yourself or Suppress Who You Are

What's more challenging than maturity is not losing yourself when becoming one. Each person has an identity separate from their relationship prior to coming into it. Because becoming one requires each individual to change, it becomes easy to lose oneself in your partner. If you allow this to happen, you can begin to resent the other person and blame them for your lack of happiness. You will easily place unrealistic expectations on them to fulfil your needs in ways that no human can. If you fail at something, you will immediately blame them for it instead of taking responsibility yourself.

Although you are becoming one, you cannot forget that you two have separate identities that come together to form a team. Each person brings something unique to the table and offers something valuable to the other person. Do not lose your value by consuming yourself in the other person. Do not let your spouse become your idol. Even couples that work together, do ministry together, or spend a great deal of time together need some time apart to refresh themselves. It's important for each spouse to have their own identity within the marriage without allowing the marriage itself to become a mask for each partner to hide behind.

For example, you may be a wife, but that is just one of your roles. You are also a daughter, sister, friend, mother, dancer, musician, baker, cook, or teacher. Allow yourself time to do things that bring you happiness as an individual and that allow you to express your purpose. Remember that happiness is always a temporary state of being caused by a series of actions, interactions, or events. Happiness comes and goes quickly. Happiness is not to be confused with joy which is an inner feeling of peace despite your temporary emotional state.

Lastly, it's also important to remember that your marriage is *your* marriage and not your parents' marriage or your in-laws' marriage. Never allow someone else's expectations of their marriage to define yours.

Play Your Role but Live Out Your Purpose

Moving forward, my husband and I challenged ourselves daily to meet each other's needs, recommit to each other, and do whatever it took to make our relationship work. Yet even when my needs were often met, I still felt like something was missing. No matter how hard we tried to make things work, I was always was left feeling empty and void. I knew that he loved me, and I knew that I loved him and our children, but I did not understand what was wrong. I understood that I was a wife and a mother, but these were roles and not an all-encompassing picture of who I really was on the inside. I felt like I was trapped, suffocating, and I did not know what to do.

Naively, I began to resent my husband and blame him for my voids. I thought that he was not loving me enough or showing me the type of affection that I needed. But when he repeatedly pointed out that he did exactly what I asked of him, I found something else to ask him to do. We were on the endless circle trying to please one another without understanding the underlying problem. NEWS FLASH! *It was an identity issue.* No one person, man, husband, friend, sister, mother, or any role could fill the void that I was experiencing. It was a void only God could fill with His supernatural power. However, I was blind to this because I did not understand my identity or the unconditional love of God.

Because I did not know how to receive God's love, I did not know how to live in it or how to properly give it. Not only was my love based on conditions, but my ability to love was limited because I did not know my identity. Therefore, I could not truly love myself in a healthy way and could not *truly* love anyone else.

As a result, I looked within my marriage and my family relationships for identity clarification and purpose. Subsequently, I was left cleaving to roles and titles such as wife, mother, friend, and sister, all of which left me feeling void, hollow, and unfulfilled. I knew that these roles held a special place in my heart and in the heart of God, but I quickly learned that they were not my sole purpose.

Being a wife and a mother were earthly roles and these duties did not distinguish me from any other wife or mother. What I mean is, any woman can become a great mother and wife without being a Christian. What makes our responsibility different is that when we are filled with God's Spirit, we have the responsibility to steward the calling of our children's lives and to fulfill our duties in a Godly way. This applies to both husbands and wives. If we are not living and operating in our purpose, it will be more difficult, if not impossible, to teach our children the same principles. We cannot settle for simply being a mother and a wife or a father and a husband and make our earthy responsibilities our calling. We can do more.

Did I say settle? Yes, I did, but bear with me. I am not in any way saying that being a wife and a mother or being a husband and a father is not difficult, challenging, or a job in itself. Trust me, I know how demanding these roles are. However, these roles are only a **part** of who we are. It does not take supernatural power to fulfill these roles in simplicity, and this is what I am referring to when I say "settling."

By no means am I saying that you don't need God in order to be a good mother, wife, father or husband. However, God has called many of us to do something more outside of these titles. This may not apply to everyone, but it's important to understand your identity so that you do not become lost in your earthly roles. Many times, when we are unclear about our purpose and we get married and have children, we assume that this must be our only responsibility. We may be rejected, feeling out of place in our community or churches, or do not understand why God put us on this earth, and so we lose ourselves in our natural roles.

Do not forfeit your God-ordained destiny because you do not know who you are meant to be. Do not settle in natural roles and forfeit your spiritual calling. Learn what God has called you to do supernaturally outside of your earthy roles. This calling will necessitate the supernatural power of God. It will require you to balance your family responsibility and your ministry in serving Him. God does not want you to neglect any of your responsibilities, so balance and wisdom is essential to executing His will for your life. Seek God to reignite the purposeful passions that He put inside you to advance His kingdom. Remember, one day your children will move out of your home and begin lives of their own. What will you do then? What is your purpose then? If you have spent all of your time in only those familiar roles, what will be next for you? It's important to explore these thoughts and seek God intently for *His* will for your life.

A friend and I were having this very discussion when she revealed to me that she feared that if she worked in ministry serving God, she would not have time to be a good mother to her children or wife to her spouse. She was not seeking what God had called her to do because she felt that being a mother and a wife was enough. I explained to her that her roles as a wife and a mother were important to God, but if she forfeited her destiny by idolizing her natural roles, she would be forfeiting a part of herself that God wanted to develop.

She reminded me of countless examples of both men and women who focused on ministry and neglected their families, and their children suffered the consequences. I reminded her that just because we have witnessed many examples of ministry and family done wrong, does not mean that God does not have an opinion about it or that He has not created a "right way" to do it. I believe that as a married person, we should devote our time to God first, then to family, then to ministry. You may disagree with this order but no matter what, we must prioritize what is important to God. Family is important to Him, but this does not mean that we should neglect any of our other responsibilities.

If you are in a romantic relationship or are in the process of becoming one with another person, you must understand that God has called all of us to a purpose, and we do not have an option to forfeit that call under any circumstance. Even if you are in a platonic friendship, are dating, or are single, you cannot allow "purpose" to remain in embryonic form for the sake of maintaining a relationship. A prophet once said that your purpose is the only reason why you exist. If you do not obey God and do what He has called you to do, He has no obligation to give you your next breath and to keep you alive. Your purpose is why you are still living. It was created for you to advance the kingdom of God. Forfeiting your purpose is surrendering your need to exist.

What You Do vs. Who You Are!

There is a significant difference between what you do and who you are. When you define your identity around what you do only, you will feel insecure, threatened, and out of place when you meet someone who does exactly what you do but better. Your identity is not what you do. Rather, it encompasses who you are in God.

What should you do when you realize that you are **not** what you do? Many people will take the first step and acknowledge that they know they are not what they do. They will say that they are "*more*," and have more to offer, and are more valuable than the things they can offer. However, simply acknowledging the facts is not enough to change them. This is especially true, if you are verbally communicating that you are **not** what you do, but your everyday behavior demonstrates that you believe the exact opposite. We have all heard that actions speak louder than words. It is true. First, once you understand that you are not what you do, you must realize that you will always be God's son or daughter. Even though He has designed you with a unique identity expression and has included your gifts, skills, and talents, never mistake those expressions as your identity.

For example, I went through several periods in my life where I was unemployed. Typically, it was after I finished a degree program and was in a period of transition. Being a natural problem-solver and planner, not having a job made me feel like my value was diminished. I felt that since I was not contributing to solving any problems or creating solutions, I was living beneath my potential. I missed the ability to earn money and those cherished feelings of accomplishment.

Even though I was a stay-at-home mom, I kept busy with housework, raising my children, professional and personal development, studying, and learning more about God, but I still felt like I needed to work. I desperately craved an outlet where I could learn more, grow, and express my skills professionally. Still, I had to learn that the outlet itself is not where my value was established.

Knowing this, I still spent years in job after job, career after career, living in a dissatisfied state despite earning plenty of money. This was because I was seeking a career to validate my worth, my existence, and my skills. It took time for me to recognize that no company could afford my true intrinsic value or establish it. Being a Christian means that my value had been established and paid for with the priceless blood of Jesus Christ. No company offer, no matter how great or small, could validate or diminish my true worth. This was liberating for me to discover in my personal journey.

Instead of seeking a job for validation, I should have been seeking what skills I could learn from the career and what the role or position could offer me in terms of growth and development. Would it challenge me to grow and develop outside of my comfort zone? Would it force me to face any fears? Would it teach me leadership skills? What I really needed to do was to discover God's idea about me. I needed to ask myself several questions such as: What does God want me to know or learn? In what areas does He desire for me to be challenged and grow?

I know that I did not want to work for someone else the rest of my life, but I needed the necessary skills and experience before I could manage and operate a successful business of my own. Nevertheless,

I needed to learn to follow the instructions given in Matthew 6:33 which instructs us to "seek first the kingdom of God and his righteousness." This was important because not seeking God and His kingdom first meant that I was allowing my career to become my idol. As a default, my career became a place of comfort and validation in place of God fulfilling those areas. Since we should only seek deep validation from God, seeking validation, confirmation, and authenticity in the wrong places will inadvertently lead to idolatry.

This example demonstrated that the test was not about my job or career but about aligning my heart with God's idea about me. He sees me through precise lenses and views me as His daughter. By seeking validation in a career, I was forfeiting my privilege as His daughter and diminishing His gift of inheritance. By becoming his daughter, I inherited all rights of His priestly kingdom. Therefore, I have access to everything that belongs to the King. Once I understood this, my intrinsic value was increased because I began to walk in the freedom of knowing that I had already been accepted by God. Everything else is a bonus.

So in seeking a career, several questions that we may need to ask ourselves are: Why this job or this role? Is this job consistent with the idea that God has about me? Do I know what ideas God has about me; and if not, am I actively seeking to find out? Are the ideas that I believe God has about me authenticated in His Word or backed by Scripture? By applying and accepting this job, role, or position, am I seeking to fulfill selfish ambition and my own personal goals, or am I consciously taking this job because I know it will help me grow and develop me according to God's ideas and thereby benefit God's kingdom?

What are the skills that this new role and position will teach me? Are these skills consistent with what I want to learn? Am I behaving in a way that is consistent with God's idea about me or am I settling for convenience? Am I simply flirting with every opportunity, or am I exercising discretion because I know my God-given worth? Am I afraid to start over if necessary because I have been going or growing in the wrong direction?

After answering these questions, a target should begin to develop. You will begin to have clarity concerning if your efforts have been going in the direction that is right for you and your identity. This process allowed me to understand what it really meant to "seek first the kingdom of God and His righteousness." I needed to ask myself if what I was doing, if what I was after, if what I was focused on accomplishing was in direct response or correlation to advancing Kingdom priorities? Are the things that I was seeking helping me to advance or partake in God's kingdom in an intentional, meaningful way?

Sometimes we yearn for things so much that we justify seeking them and create a noble motive for why we are doing what we are doing. I had to ensure that I was not making an excuse by stating that "if I earn more money, I will be able to give more to God's kingdom because any job or business venture has the potential to increase my income." Instead, I needed to ascertain whether this particular goal was going to help me work toward advancing the kingdom with intention. I had to realize that God was not looking for me to become a glorified volunteer or for me to offer Him more monetary donations. He would rather me do what He has called me to do.

When you are seeking directions for your next move in life, whether it be to volunteer in a new role in your local church, join a nonprofit organization, further your education, get a new job, or even become a business owner, always ask yourself if what you are going after directly and not casually connects you with God's Kingdom priorities. Always ensure that you are not being motivated by the urge to seek validation, approval, or acceptance. The root of these issues is a lack of identity. Ensure that you are also not motivated by wealth, money, prominence, position, recognition, fame, or esteem.

Ask yourself if you going to make yourself available to kingdom priorities. This process will require humility and will challenge you to be honest with yourself. Every individual must separate what they do from who they are and even carefully scrutinize every motive. This will ensure that you will be able to truly uncover identity, purpose, and kingdom priorities.

Wishful Thinking

What you desire reveals what you believe about yourself. When you are experiencing an identity crisis, it's important to get to the bottom of who you are by examining the things that you crave. It's equally important to determine how you are approaching God for answers.

In the past, I approached God with my desires. I frequently asked God to reveal "His will" while secretly wishing for my desires *to be* His will, ultimately asking Him to bless me in the things that I wanted. Of course, God is not fooled by such folly. We often deceive ourselves by playing the game of wishful thinking. Habitually, we make choices and decisions without consulting God and then later ask God to bless those decisions. God is not obligated to bless you in something that He never intended. We must crucify our desires and ask Him to give us what we should desire.

An identity crisis should be treated as a destiny emergency. To neutralize the threat, we must be willing to allow God to perform surgery on our desires. The goal is to transform our desires to what He wants, in order for us to walk in complete obedience to Him. Psalm 37:4 reminds us that if we delight ourselves in the Lord, He will give us what we should desire: "the desires of our heart." This verse does always point to God giving us everything we want but instead expresses that He will articulate the types of things we should want in the first place. He will literally give us His desires, and if His desires become ours, then we will be able to walk in complete obedience to Him.

The process of obedience and completely surrendering your desires to learn what God wants for you will support accurate identity revelation. However, while you must simultaneously seek to understand your potential, your identity, and your gifts, you must also seek to align yourself with God's ideas for you according to His pace, rhythm, and His timing.

Stop and Reflect

I hope you have your journal or pad of paper ready...

1. Identify the areas where you have suppressed yourself. This may be in regard to your creativity, your abilities, your personality, your roles, and your passions. Write down why you think you suppressed yourself in these areas.
2. Were you able to control the situation? Why or why not?
3. In the future, what situations will it be difficult for you to allow "you" to be present?
4. What preparations can you make now in order to not suppress yourself when the temptation comes again in the future?
5. Because you understand that you are not what you do, begin to make a list of all of your roles, and next to each one, write "this is a role and not my purpose."
6. Identify any areas of wishful thinking. Have you made plans without consulting God and then asked Him to bless your ideas? Challenge yourself to release your own desires for His will.
7. If you have already overcome suppressing who you really are, what steps did you take to achieve that freedom? Acknowledge the success and determine in what other ways you can continue to grow and be fully "you."

Lost

Hastily, I jumped into my car, buckled my seatbelt, and started my engine.

Eager to leave with a tank full of gas, I sensed no immediate apprehension.

I started driving down the road quickly because I had someplace new to be.

I was excited about this new adventure because of all the sights I would see.

It should only take me a few days, and to my new location I would arrive.

I had a new car, fair directions, and though solo, I knew I would survive.

I was driving at a reasonable speed with expected stops along the way,

But as I traveled each mile, I seemed to end up in an unfamiliar place.

My destination was clear, but the directions became quite confusing.

Should I go back, turn left or right, or should I keep on cruising?

My map did not show this fork in the road with two signs reading detour,

Gripping my steering wheel close, I stayed the course, but I still felt so unsure.

In a panic, I decided to go left, because I figured… I'm smart, I can find my way.

But on this road, there were large boulders, narrow curves, and mountains to navigate.

Laser focused, I peered through my windshield, questioning my 20/20 vision,

I was now approaching a cliff head-on and I knew I needed to make a quick decision.

On the brink of disaster, my pounding heart grew constricted and felt tight,

So I turned sharply left, skidded on two wheels, and swirled faster than light.

I plummeted in the air, then crashed on all four wheels, just escaping a catastrophe.

I wish I had taken my time, not left in a hurry, and perhaps eluded this calamity.

On the new road, I was even more lost with no clue how to get back on track,

I did not even know from which direction I came, so I certainly could not turn back.

Suddenly I was feeling the cold silence of being alone and on my own.

This new adventure felt so great at first, but now I did not even know my way home.

So, I kept traveling forward on this road called left, knowing I was going the wrong direction,

But I kept my pride intact because it was my defense, my only shield of protection.

My distorted vision was blurred further by the rain that began to downpour,

I needed help, I was lost, but in this quiet place, who could I call for?

In a panic, I tried to phone a friend, but my phone did not have a signal,

Was I really lost? Was I really alone? Yes, it was undeniably official!

I would have asked a stranger for help, but not a soul was nearby,

Blackness surrounded me, silence engulfed me, and I felt quite mystified.

Bewildered by this entire voyage, I lost myself completely,

I didn't know where I was, what to do, or who could save me.

My next decision could prove to be one of life or death because I could not see,

But unexpectedly, I seen a light and heard a voice say, "Come closer,
    it's me."
I drove closer and closer even though I was blinded by great drops
    of rain,
I seen an arrow pointing and a sign that read "This way, you'll never
    be the same!"

Chapter 3

Identity Road Trip

Are You Lost?

Have you ever taken a long trip or traveled to a new destination and gotten lost? You may have had the right directions but there were unexpected detours or changes in the road that were difficult to navigate? Or, through no fault of your own, you were required to go a route that you didn't intend? Have you ever been driving and missed a turn or drove past your exit? Did attempting to figure out how to get back on track become stressful if not impossible? Exploring your identity is like going on a long road trip. Without adequate preparation, direction, or tools, you may never reach your destination.

There are several things that make a road trip much easier such as planning, not rushing, and pacing yourself. You must have adequate directions, have properly packed your bags, have reliable transportation and gas, and have determined the time it will take you to travel. It takes patience, endurance, stamina, and laser focus to keep your destination in sight. You must be well rested, not become weary too soon, and take rests when needed. If you do not adequately prepare for your trip, you may end up lost or experience delay or disaster.

Discovering your identity without adequate tools such as prayer, knowing God's directions, and hearing His voice will certainly make the process difficult. Having an underdeveloped relationship with Him will also decrease your ability to navigate challenges along the way. Although your identity itself is not exactly a destination but an ever-evolving you, it's important to know how to have sufficient resources to begin unearthing the "truest you" God created you to be. It is also important to be healthy emotionally and psychologically in order to recognize the difference between your emotions, feelings, and strong convictions and God's plan for your life. We cannot make up our own directions and expect not to get lost along the way. We also cannot go in the wrong direction or create our own plan and ask God to bless it. It is better to know His plan in advance and follow it as precisely as possible.

Getting lost is one of the most awkward feelings you can experience. It is common to feel out of place and to experience fear, anxiety, and worry. You easily feel out of your depth, embarrassed, and distressed. Living in an inauthentic identity is akin to being lost; it is like driving down a long road without clear-cut directions. You may be prone to make decisions grounded in your opinion, impulse, or convenience, without clear consideration or insight. Or you may be driving down a road with the wrong directions altogether. So, although each point on your map is clearly indicated, if your destination is not properly marked, you will expend more time wandering, making unnecessary stops, experiencing needless delays, and wind up exhausting valuable resources.

This is can be both dangerous and reckless. When you are lost, it is easy to take your cues from your environment and to use those as symbols to give you direction instead of reading from a roadmap. God has a plan for each individual, and the roadmap for your life has been created by Him. Often these details can be found in His written Word as well as in learning to hear His voice more intently. Seeking to unearth what His plans are for your life will give you access to your authentic identity.

As mentioned before, this requires developing an intimate bond with your Creator. This is because seeking your identity apart from God wastes time. It is equivalent to driving down a road blind without His detailed blueprint. The more you understand who God is, the more you will understand how and why He created you. Never forget that **you** are made in *His* likeness.

Lost: Wasting Time and Resources

One of the most exasperating things about being lost is wasting precious time. Time is one commodity that, if wasted, can never be reacquired. It is gone forever. Living in a counterfeit identity is traveling like a lost person. Unless it is revealed to you, you will persistently drive in circles on a road that will never help you identify your true purpose. Even if there are signs that indicate you are out of place, you will miss these key indicators because you will process them as the norm instead of as a signal to turn around.

As mentioned before, knowing your identity paves the way for you to understand your purpose. Trying to discover your purpose when your identity is unclear is like carrying a blank check with the ability to withdraw any amount, without knowing what bank has issued the check, and without knowing what bank will accept your deposit. Its value is diminished by your lack of clarity. Living a purposeless life devalues your existence, permits your gifts to remain uncultivated, and fuels frustration to your innate design. Frustrated people often live their lives frustrating others because they are confused about who they are.

Have you ever met someone who thought they could really sing, except it was obvious to everyone else that the sound they were hearing coming out of their windpipes was not the sound that everyone else was hearing? Not only is it frustrating for the person to receive negative reviews about their singing, it's equally frustrating to everyone else who has to sit and suffer listening to the awful tunes. When you are in your rightful place and living in your right identity, you can focus on strengthening, learning, and growing in your purpose, utilizing your innate skill set. You'll devote less time in confusion and less time "trying out" roles instead of reserving your energy for your purpose.

Lost people inherently squander resources. If begin your road trip with a full tank of gas and get lost, not only may you not reach your destination at all, you may not have enough fuel to get to the next gas station or rest stop. God has given each person a certain amount of days to accomplish the tasks He has set out for them to complete while on earth. None of us will live on this earth forever. You may be equipped with a certain amount of energy, zeal, and youth to prepare you for destiny. However, if you pour out your energy in the wrong areas, you often will be too tired to start over again and muster enough energy to go in the right direction.

I'm not saying that you can't start over or shouldn't if you have to, but most would agree that if make good choices early on, you can save yourself some headaches later. Don't be that person who waits until they are seventy-five to decide that they weren't truly living in their purpose or authentic identity. Please do not waste your time, youth, or energy in the wrong identity. If you have not discovered what God has deposited in you for your destiny, begin immediately to seek Him and His direction and align with His purpose. Once you discover the next steps, get moving right way. Eliminate your excuses and find your "why."

Lost and Stubborn: The Cave of Idolatry

Many have heard of the person who won't stop and ask for directions. We may think to ourselves that a person who refuses to ask for help is in the worst type of situation because they are blinded by their own need to figure everything out. However, I believe that a person who does not know that they are lost sits in a worse position than a person who will not ask for help.

Typically, both scenarios are the result of pride, because like any lost person will tell you, they are just so close to figuring it out themselves. They are seeking the gratification, self-satisfaction of knowing that they are in control, and the relief that having control brings them. However, a person who does not know that they are lost will wander aimlessly, going in circles without realizing that they are wasting their own time and energy. They are blinded by their own stubbornness, their need to be right, and their need to be in control, *every...single...time*. When we are stubborn and worship our own opinion, we enter into idolatry.

First Samuel 15:23 states that "rebellion is as the sin of witch-craft, and stubbornness is as iniquity and idolatry" (KJV). When you are lost in your identity or in your clarity, it's essential to remain teachable and humble. There are countless people who forget this principle and refuse to subject themselves to teaching that is above their own level. Thinking of yourself more highly than you ought to think will lead to conceitedness, delay, and self-destruction. It will also prevent you from making sound decisions because your ability to be objective will be obscured by your ego.

It is much easier for God to communicate to a meek person who has a ready ear to listen than a person who continuously seeks God but also seeks to control their situation. They are comfortable being self-reliant, self-willed, and self-influenced. God is not impressed with our self-reliance and our ability to solve our own problems every time. Not only has he given us permission to ask Him for help, He encourages us to do just that. In Isaiah 55:8–9, He reminds us that His thoughts are not our thoughts and His ways not like our own but much higher (KJV). When we are not lost, we should default to delighting in God's ways, His thoughts, and His plans more than our own.

It's on Your Map: Linking Faith and Patience

God often provides a full picture before He ever reveals the smallest details. He regularly leaves us with a map without a legend or key. It allows us to see a beginning and a destination, without really revealing the steps in between. However, God builds our map utilizing faith and patience. It's no secret that we all need to grow in our faith. Even though we often ask God to give us more faith or pray for more faith, the Scriptures are very clear about the way in which faith is grown.

Romans 10:17 states, "So then faith cometh by hearing, and hearing by the Word of God." It's important to note that many scholars agree that the phrase "Word of God" in this scripture is not referring to the "logos" or the written collection of Scripture as a whole but the *rhema* Word of God.[3] This is significant because what this

---

[3] R. Watson Jr. in an online lecture titled "Foundations Class, Part 4: Faith" (presented via Zoom, July 1, 2019).

does <u>not</u> mean is that when you open the Bible, you can simply read a collection of scriptures and then receive an increase of faith as a byproduct of simply reading. In this context, "the Word of God" referring to *rhema* emphasizes that a revelation is obtained from the "Word," which is Jesus Himself (according to John 1:1–14).

Although a revelation can also be obtained from the *logos* or collection of scriptures themselves, the main emphasis of *rhema* is to receive a revelation at a greater level of clarity because one grows in their understanding of what Jesus has spoken. When you hear what Christ has spoken and decided about you, you then formulate a picture or a vision. Once you have seen that picture, it provides hope and substance to your faith. This then means that faith does not come by praying for it, declaring it, or simply desiring it. It comes through revelation of hearing God's Word, which is understanding with greater clarity what God's vision is, what He has spoken, and what He has desired for you and for your life.

When your faith is being built, there is usually a situation that God will use in order to bring about greater clarity and revelation. This situation is usually a lesson rooted deeply in patience. No one likes to wait! It is our natural human nature to be impatient. Patience is a hardening process, meaning that it is a repetitive process of testing and retesting until the concept of total trust in God takes precedence and is realized as a permanent war tactic.

Patience forces you to deny your fleshly desires and human nature and requires you to (1) renew your mind; (2) reset; and (3) realign with the will of God. Patience hardens you like a callus. We know that calluses are the result of repeated friction of the skin, where the skin thickens and hardens in order to protect itself from injury.[4] Tests of patience force you to continuously apply faith to situations without getting an immediate result. Because instantaneous results are always desired, when they do not occur quickly after having already applied absolute faith in God, the result is direct disappointment. When disappointment finds rest in the mind, fear and doubt

---

[4] *Oxford Dictionary*, s.v. "callus" (accessed August 24, 2020, from https://www.lexico.com/definition/callus).

often grow in its place. This is why you must continuously learn to reapply faith each time you feel disappointed. James 1:3–4 states "the trying of your faith worketh patience" (KJV).

In a test of patience, your faith is tried again and again and again, often for the same situation in a different presentation. This process usually brings you to a breaking point where you want to give up and give in to your emotions. You will want to avoid repeated disappointment by believing that it's much easier to lower your expectations and not have any faith at all.

It's easier to try to figure out a way to do it on your own or to believe that God is not really going to come through for you. It's easier to give up hope than it is to endure the pain of having to wait and live in expectation. However, the instant you want to give up is the very moment in which you need to reapply your faith with expectation.

It is easy to apply faith to something and then carry an attitude of "if it happens it happens, but if it doesn't it doesn't." However, this is not genuine faith. It's not real faith unless there is real, high, immediate expectation. In expectation, there is always a sense of urgency or imminence out of belief that anything could happen at any second. If you have a nonchalant relationship with the immediacy of your expectation, your faith will be dull and will have be tested and retested in order to be sharpened.

Even though what you are believing for may not happen right away, the goal is to keep expectation and faith high, regardless of the timeline. This will teach you real patience and help you learn to build up more faith, block by block, until there is no "Plan B" or doubt in your mind that what you're believing God for is imminent.

Patience teaches you to examine your motives for why you want something and helps you discover if your plans, vision, and goals are in the way of what God really wants for you. You cannot please God without faith, according to Hebrews 11:6. This is important to develop in your identity because you cannot relate to God without faith. "Faith," says R. Watson Jr., "is the vehicle that God uses to get us to the future."

Speeding Past Your Exit: Patience

One of the hardest lessons to learn for any person is patience. Have you ever seen a baby cry at the top of its lungs for a bottle? They are so hungry and focused on communicating their hunger that they cannot see their parent preparing the bottle for them. Their eyes are squinted and welled up with angry tears as their lungs bellow their demands. Sometimes, despite seeing the bottle being prepared, they simply cannot wait, and so in their frustration, they fly into an outburst. They do not understand that soon they will be able to eat to their satisfaction.

This is exactly how we behave when we have to wait for something God has promised us. We are too busy squinting our eyes to see with clear vision. We are too busy whining, crying, and complaining to see the promise has already been prepared for us. We are too busy having outbursts full of disappointment, doubt, and frustration to realize what God has right before our eyes.

Patience is the act of holding on to expectations despite feeling stalled. It's also the act of enduring pain and frustration without retaliating with unbelief, doubt, pouting, and murmuring. A wise person once said that patience is not just about the ability to wait but the ability to keep a right attitude about the waiting process. When you holler, bawl, and scream like the hungry infant for God to give you your desired milk, you show your immaturity. You are blinded by your hunger pangs and your cravings for answers, all while your Father in heaven is preparing your way. Patience requires you to be integral, builds your character, deepens your level of faith, and helps to clear your head of doubt.

Discovering your identity requires both patience and endurance because you may not always perceive the key indicators that will reveal your purpose and destiny. Persistent searching and examination coupled with the scrutiny of the Word of God can uncover those missing links you were searching for. It is common to detest waiting because perpetual anticipation forces us to be vulnerable to the unexpected and makes us uncomfortable. However, unexpected phenomena are the very things that strengthen us, reveal our character, and lead us further into true identity exploration.

How many times have you made a great discovery or revelation by accident? You had an original plan, but that plan was disrupted by an unexpected incident that led you to a better direction. God executes His plan in ways that we don't always understand. Allowing Him to take the lead and teaching yourself to be patient will better prepare you for everything that He has designed for you.

Speeding Out of Alignment

Have you ever been in a hurry and forgot a few things that you needed for your trip, like the address to your location? Or have you ever left something incredibly important and had to purchase it when you reached your destination? Lost people rush and become increasingly impatient. When you rush, it's easy to make unnecessary, costly mistakes. It makes the process more frustrating and tedious.

Learning your identity is a process that cannot be rushed. Rushing the process can easily get you off course just as listening to bad advice can detour you. Sometimes you learn that you have been living as a counterfeit and have spent much of your time and resources in the wrong areas. When you discover that you have not been living as your truest self, you immediately want to go full speed ahead to get realigned with what God has called you to become. This is a great first step but remember how important it is to know the voice of God in order to prevent yourself from becoming more lost and confused.

Aggressively pursuing God and your purpose will eventually lead to destiny. In the meantime, God will begin to build your character, your integrity, and your gifts, all of which will make your purpose easier to fulfil. If you get to your purpose prior to God building your character, you can cause shipwreck and end up abandoning your destiny altogether. Quality is usually valued over quantity, so ensure that you are going at a pace that allows you to develop with strength and resilience.

God's Pace with God's Grace

You must know that you are not meant to do everything alone. However, sometimes seeking clarification in your purpose will require you to steer clear of certain people. Sometimes you may have to separate for good from those who are toxic; other times, you may have to separate for a season. Do not allow your relationships with others to determine your direction or your pace. You need God's direction, His guidance, and His voice to provide clarity in your identity-discovery process.

Every step you take without God's voice is one that reinforces the counterfeit you and impedes your progress. God has a set timing, rhythm, and pace in which He wants to accomplish things in your life. It's important to remember that God has set this pace and there is nothing you can do to speed it up or slow it down. Bolting too fast in one direction without God's instructions is a recipe for disaster. You will end up aggravated, disoriented, and feeling like you have failed yourself and God.

No matter which direction you start on, you'll always come across bumps in the road and unexpected happenings of life that can divert your course. It is essential to know how to get realigned when you find yourself lost. This is why God has poured His grace into us so that when we need Him, He will help. Also, if possible, seek counsel from godly people around you who can help you navigate those bumpy roads. No matter how much you think you already know, there is always more to learn. Sometimes you can learn from making mistakes, but if there are avoidable pitfalls, make a conscious effort to steer clear of them. Remember, remain in God's grace and His timing for the pace of your life.

Weariness: A Rest Stop of Fear

Sometimes when you get lost, you feel like you just need to stop and take a rest. You feel overwhelmed and burdened. Stopping feels like the best option. Sometimes when you feel lost, you will become impatient, and this impatience leads to weariness. Weariness often leads to fear.

In First Samuel, chapter thirteen, we learn about the battle that Saul was going to face against the Philistines. The Philistines had around three thousand chariots and about six thousand soldiers, and the people of Israel felt distressed, outnumbered, and overwhelmed. Samuel was supposed to meet Saul at Gilgal, but after waiting for Samuel for seven days, Saul became impatient and fearful that Samuel would not come. Saul's anxiousness and impatience led him to take matters into his own hands and he illegally offered up sacrifices to the Lord. This action was in direct disobedience to the word of God and resulted in Saul losing his authority to reign. The unfortunate timing of Saul's decision was underscored by the fact that Samuel had been very close to arriving when Saul offered the illegal sacrifice.

Time and time again, our impatience encourages us to take matters into our own hands, often leading to disastrous results. Therefore, it is critical that we wait on the Lord for our identity development and confirmation. Jumping too soon in one direction can lead to disobedience and create grievous situations. It is when we feel lost that it is essential to exercise the greatest patience. Do not allow your inability to wait on God lead you to make decisions out of fear. Only tragic consequences can result from swift and hasty decision-making.

God cares about you and has not forgotten about you or your situation. In Romans 8:25, it says that "we should hope for that which we cannot see and with patience continue to wait for it." God is going to answer you if you simply wait on Him. Even when you decide that maybe you need to rest and stop moving, use this rest stop to press into God's voice and God's will more intently. Do not allow this rest stop to stall you or keep you in fear paralysis.

When you are lost, it's important to understand that you are not in charge of leading yourself. God, like any great leader, understands the principles and the tools developed in patience. Sometimes we may feel lost in our identity because we are not sure which way to go and we don't want to wait to develop the tools needed for our destiny. For example, wise, experienced leaders can astutely discern inexperienced followers who may want to become leaders themselves. However, if the inexperienced have not developed the tools necessary to lead, and if they cannot endure the pain and the burden that follow after leading, they will exhaust themselves and will not last.

At times, God permits us to get lost as an expression of His will to teach us to seek Him more deeply. He understands the value in waiting and the tools and experience we will develop during this process. If Saul had waited patiently for Samuel, his story may have ended differently. Some things, like developing useful tools, only occur when you are forced to wait on God. This is a process that cannot be expedited.

To illustrate this example further, consider that it takes years for a baby to develop all its teeth as it grows from an infant to an adolescent. Even when baby teeth develop, those teeth fall out to make room for bigger, stronger, adult teeth. This process of development takes time. Even then, children have to be taught how to properly care for the new teeth once they grow in, otherwise, decay, gum disease, or cavities may develop and destroy them. Even with proper care, teeth may grow in crooked, overcrowded, twisted, may chip, or grow in on top of each other. The environment in which the teeth grow may affect the way that they come in. New teeth may grow in and push out the old teeth, some may come out prematurely without enough room for the new teeth to come in, and some teeth may grow in odd directions on their own. Consequently, stronger tools such as braces, retainers, aligners, or even surgery may be needed to fix and realign the teeth.

God often teaches us when we are inexperienced how to acquire and develop skills that are necessary to prepare us for maturity and future development. Once the basics are mastered, we as inexperienced believers can prepare for more challenges. God in His infinite wisdom helps us to sharpen and straighten out poorly developed tools. These tools will help us chew and digest the challenges we face with greater precision, functionality, and experience. This is more than a cosmetic fix; it is a process that develops mastery, good character, and sound judgment.

During identity formulation, you will be forced to wait on God, but you must understand that God is your greatest leader. He knows how to properly sharpen, straighten, and care for you during your phases of development just as you had to learn as a child to care for your teeth. Because He is a good father, He teaches us to brush our teeth, floss them, and properly rinse. In other words, He teaches us how to develop and care for the tools that we have developed in order to become more effective in serving Him and fulfilling our purpose.

It is also important to remember that during the development phases of your teeth, your body learns how to prepare for more mature digestive processes. You stomach and body changes from only being able to consume milk to being able to digest meat. Again, this is a maturity process that takes time. Acknowledging the existence of your tools, strengths, or gifts does not mean you are mature enough to use them in the most effective way. God's development process perfects you in His time. Even if it were possible to speed up the development process, it is not in your best interest because just like teeth that come in too fast without enough room, greater means to fix your poorly developed tools, will be a consequence of your impatience.

Comparison: A Rest Stop of Pride

Another indication of a lost person is someone who is stuck in comparison. There is never a need to compare your progress, success, or lack thereof with another person. Only people who are lost in their identity will focus on making evaluations and assessments about other people. Galatians 6:4 states,

> But let every person carefully scrutinize and examine and test his own conduct and his own work. He then can have the personal satisfaction and joy of doing something commendable (in itself alone) without (resorting to) boastful comparison with his neighbor. (AMPC)

Comparison breeds pride within yourself and against God. It causes you to measure yourself against others, placing yourself either above or beneath them. If above, then pride is obvious; if beneath, you are signaling to God that what He has done in your life or for you is not enough. Either way, pride is manifesting.

When we work and measure our own accomplishments, we realize that we are only in a race against our last "best" against ourselves. We can then find gratefulness and satisfaction in the things that God is doing through us and for us without comparing those things to others.

Even when people say things like "I'm glad that I'm not like this person or that person because God has done this or that for me," pride is still evident. You can be happy and grateful about what God has done or is doing for you without comparing yourself to the misfortune of others. When you are focused on your own work and your own identity, you will not have time to compare yourselves to others. You'll be able to genuinely celebrate someone else's accomplishments without mentioning your own or focusing on their deficits. You will be able to not feel like you need to have "one-up" on someone else.

There's nothing more telling than when you share with someone that you received a promotion on your job or earned a degree or some other accomplishment and they respond with "I did that too!" You will instantly become aware of that person's insecurities, possible jealousy, and pride. Sometimes within our culture, gloating is smiled upon. Although there is nothing wrong with self-celebration, it should never be done in comparison to what someone else has or has not done. A spirit of comparison frequently breeds pride, jealousy, envy, and hatred.

Lost? Me? Never!

Some may argue that they do not *feel* lost at all. They may know the way in which God has directed them, they may be walking in their complete identity, and they may have endured many processes. They may even stress that they are simply waiting for the manifestation of some part of the process. For those who feel that they are completely in line with God in every area, consider challenging yourself by asking God if there is anything about you that *you* do not know.

Is there any area that He desires to invade in order to get you to think differently about Him and about yourself? Remember how I said earlier that the most dangerous people are the people who do not even realize that they are lost in their identity? Honestly, no one has **everything** all figured out. Even when we think that we do, we must carefully examine ourselves by the Word of God, put our egos aside, and seek His will for our lives and our identity more intensely.

Sometimes, the way in which you operated previously was God-ordained but as you mature, God challenges you to take on something new and different. Even things that He wouldn't allow you to do before due to your spiritually immaturity, He may permit. You will likely face new challenges and will have to create new boundaries. God wants to mold us and shape us into the idea that He has about us, not the idea we have about ourselves. If we never allow ourselves to be open to His thoughts and His ways, we forbid Him access to change and cultivate our identity to facilitate mature growth.

Because God loves us, He does not force His will upon us; He gives us the freedom to choose whether or not we will obey Him. He gives us the opportunity to love Him unconditionally just as He loves us unconditionally. However, when we reject the idea that it is possible to be lost in our purpose, thinking we already know the way God wants to do something in us, or thinking we are so close to figuring it out ourselves, we limit our ability to hear and understand God's will for us. We must set our pride aside and authorize God to examine us more carefully.

God rarely forces His will upon us, if ever at all; we must invite Him into every area of our lives. We must humble ourselves and ask Him what our identity and purpose should look like in order to reflect Him more perfectly.

Crossing: The River of Denial

Frequently, denial approaches us like a crossroad. We have to choose to accept or deny the truth. Denial is the failure to acknowledge truth, acknowledge our emotions, or allow truth to come into consciousness.[5] Sometimes we pretend that we do not know who we are, or we run from who we are because we want to have an excuse for not becoming who we are meant to be *fully*. We run from specific instructions that God has given us, trying to hide behind our comfort zones, to avoid bucking the system around us, or the family standard, and in order to maintain the status quo.

For example, we may find ourselves in a state of denial when we are constantly looking and searching for something that doesn't exist. This is because we may have been called to build it or create it ourselves. We convince ourselves that we are not qualified to build or create something that is so much greater than what we have seen before. So instead of building, we enter a state of denial where we are self-persuaded that we have to keep looking for this new thing. We reiterate in our subconscious what we're looking for, and this in turn becomes our vision instead of God's vision. We either assume that this new vision is either already built and we must find it, or we look for someone we deem qualified to build it first and then simply follow after them. We exempt ourselves from moving forward by disqualifying ourselves.

Denial in this scenario is used as a defense mechanism to keep us from stretching outside our comfort zones and from coming into the reality of our identity and purpose, which in this case is as a pioneer. A pioneer is defined as a "person who is among the first to explore something new, a person who is among the first to research [and or] develop a new area of knowledge or activity,"[6] or a person who fosters a new movement or idea. Not everyone is called to do something that has been done before; some are called to do something new. If you find yourself lost on an identity road trip, you may have to reexamine your thoughts to see if you are in denial about something that you are specifically supposed to do.

---

[5]   *Oxford Dictionary*, s.v. "denial" (accessed on August 24, 2020, from https:// www.lexico.com/en/definition/denial).

[6]   *Oxford Dictionary*, s.v. "pioneer" (accessed on August 24. 2020 from https:// www.lexico.com/en/definition/pioneer).

You may actually know who you are meant to be but are denying it because it seems greater than you. This is why it will require God and why self-reliance will never stretch beyond our own capabilities. Once you recognize that it is only God who can disqualify you from something, only God who can launch you into something bigger than yourself, then you can bravely step out of denial and into faith to become who God already says you are. God will only ask you to surrender your vision for His because He knows what is best for you.

Avoiding the Anxiety Avalanche

"Anxiety is a state of uneasiness, worry, abnormal fear that lacks a root cause, or a sense of fear or dread without being able to specifically name its source."[7] Anxiety is a catastrophic spirit of fear that will drop on you like an avalanche.

When you become lost under the power of anxiety, it becomes increasingly difficult to look at yourself, your life, and your identity through a pure lens. This is because the ultimate goal of anxiety is to rob you of your mental stability, your ability to hear the voice of God, and your ability to be connected to God. Anxiety produces frustration, ungratefulness, anger, pride, pessimism, impatience, and robs you of your joy. We can find all of this in Philippians 4:6–8, which tells us,

> Be careful [or anxious for nothing, meaning do not worry about anything]; but in everything by prayer and supplication with thanksgiving let your requests be made known unto God. And the peace of God, which surpasses all understanding, shall keep your hearts and minds through Christ Jesus. Finally, brethren, whatsoever things are true, whatsoever things are honest, whatsoever

---

[7] As defined by Joyce Meyer in *Worry-Free Living: Trading Anxiety for Peace* (New York: FaithWords, 2016).

things are just, whatsoever things are pure, whatsoever things are lovely, whatsoever things are of
good report; if there be any virtue, and if there be
any praise, think on these things. (KJV)

If we analyze the first portion of this scripture, where it instructs us to give thanks to God while we are in prayer, and make our requests known to him; we discover that this instruction is here because when we are in anxiety and worry, we cannot be grateful. We will become so focused on what we do not have and on what is not going accord-ing to plan that we forget to thank God for what He has already done. We become more self-centered and less God-centered.

The next portion tells us that the peace of God will literally stand guard over all our thoughts and feelings. His peace will lit-erally keep our thoughts grounded and focused. This reveals to us that when we are preoccupied with worry and anxiety, we cannot control our thoughts or emotions, and therefore, we cannot walk in peace. We will literally allow our thoughts to run wild, creating false assumptions, letting negativity rule, and blaming ourselves, others, or God for our current situation.

When we review the last verse, we notice that it instructs us to think positively. This lets us know that when we are full of anxiety and worry, we cannot think positively or focus on things that are true, honest, lovely, and pure. Instead, we will be full of negativity and pessimism. If you have ever encountered a person who is nega-tive and full of pessimism, they are also likely to be full of worry and anxiety because it is the spirit of fear that produces such cynicism.

First Peter 5:6–7 says, "Humble yourselves therefore under the mighty hand of God, that he may exalt you in due time: Casting all your care upon him; for he cares for you" (KJV). In other words, "So be humble under God's powerful hand. Then he will lift you up when the right time comes. Give all your worries to him, because he cares for you" (ERV). This reveals to us that anxious people are full of pride, and are impatient because they are more concerned about their own personal timelines than God's will, and His plan for their lives. We are reminded in this scripture to remain humble, and at the right time, God will lift us up. We are to give or cast all of our cares or worries on Him. We cannot do this if we are holding on to them ourselves.

Have you ever met a person who refuses to smile, and when asked, they say that they say that they don't have anything to smile about? This is the result of being robbed of internal joy by the enemy. Proverbs 15:13 says, "A merry heart makes a cheerful countenance: but by sorrow of the heart the spirit is broken" (KJV). This tells us that, just like in the children's song, if you are happy and you know it, your face will definitely show it.

Proverbs 15:15 says, "All the days of the afflicted are evil: but he that is of a merry heart hath a continual feast" (KJV). The ERV translation says, "Life is always hard for the poor, but the right attitude can turn it into a party." This scripture lets us know that anxiety makes life hard and robs you of the joy, the "party," or the peace God wants all of us to have in life.

Do not fall for the trick of anxiety or fear in general. When you are full of any type of fear, it will become more difficult to piece together your identity and your purpose. I will discuss fear in more detail in a later chapter, but what I want to point out here is that anxiety robs you of a close connection with God. A great book to read on anxiety if you are struggling in this area is Joyce Meyer's *Worry-Free Living: Trading Anxiety for Peace.*

Stop and Reflect

It's time to journal again; I hope you are ready!

1. Acknowledge all of the areas in your life where you feel that you do not have all of the answers. This is literally stating that you don't know the "whys" (why did God allow this happen, why did this happen in this way, what was the point?). Then begin to ask God why and listen for His answers. If you don't hear anything right away, it is okay to continue to make a practice of asking God. Some people are afraid to ask God questions, but Jesus told us in

Matthew 7:7–8, "Ask, and it shall be given you; seek, and ye shall find; knock, and it shall be opened unto you: For every one that asks receives; and he that seeks, finds; and to him that knocks, it shall be opened" (KJV). This is giving us permission to ask and seek Him out for answers. He has answers to every question you could ever ask. Patiently await His answers after asking because He is a rewarder of them who diligently seek Him (Hebrews 11:6).

2. Carefully comb through all of the areas of your identity where you have questions, insecurities, and pain. Identify why, if at all, any of these areas have held you back, caused you to become impatient, guarded, prideful, or weary. Make a conscious effort to give God these burdens and free yourself from their weight.

I Am Not You

I remember the hot sting of your betrayal when I scraped my knee roller-skating as a young child. Then, our relationship wasn't in full bloom and I wasn't aware of your trickery and guile.

I knew that I had made a mistake because I had fallen to the ground and gotten hurt. I didn't know about your plan to eat me alive and devour me as tasty dessert.

As I grew older, the hatred I felt for you was stronger than any love I've felt before.

My fourth-grade teacher asks, "What's one hundred divided by four?" "Twenty," I say, "Wrong," and my pride falls flat on the floor.

You see, the question was simple, how could I get it wrong, how could I make this mistake? How could I be tricked into playing a game I wasn't given the rules to play?

You choked me with your death-grip, squeezing the breath out of my life, suffocating my freedom, while infiltrating my very DNA.

You force-fed me hypocrisy, making me believe our bond was normal, while spoon-feeding me an embellished blanket of lies. You covered my blindness in a cloak of tenderness, creating a passion that left me brainwashed and hypnotized.

You told me you were my friend, made me believe you needed me, we were like family, and suddenly we became identical twins. It was as if you became me and I became you and I had no choice but to accept your lifeblood, and allow you to come in.

What I didn't know is how much you wanted to become a part of me, to be in my blood, and in my veins. You wanted me to fall, remain stuck, and drown in the quicksand of my misery and shame.

In young adulthood, we meet again, and I hear you knocking at the entrance of my front door. But this time you're disguised, as a charming young man, with a sweet smile, looking for more.

Oooo Mistake! I feel your burn as you clothe me with kisses of tangled barbwire. The treachery of your deceit, the emptiness travels deep, you fire several shots at me.

And oh, how I wish your gun would have misfired.

Now, Mistake, I'm carrying life, you and I are engaged, and my mind is in a tug of war? Do I keep the life inside of me, marry the man beside me, or end it all with twenty-five pills or more?

Mistake, I know who you are now; we're quite acquainted, and I feel you in my dying soul. I allowed you to come in, strangle me, overpower me, and burrow a deep black hole.

Am I naïve? Am I foolish? Or, are you just too cunning? Am I your prey, is this a game of sport, or were my feelings just ripe for your hunting?

Since we're together now, I decided to move forward, get married, and start a new life. But you know the routine, why not wreak havoc on my marriage, promote confusion, destruction, and create unending strife?

I try so hard to say the right thing, to be the perfect person, perfect parent, and to live the perfect life. Does my grief bring you pleasure, in my heartache you find treasure, do my errors disqualify me from being a good mother and wife?

I'm tired of these mind games, I am hot with anger, boiling in thick agony, and numb inside of this straitjacket called stress. The ice of your laughter cannot cool this disaster that you call our relationship, it's really a cryptic cyanide process.

Oh Mistake, or should I say Mistakes, because now you're plural, more than one, and you're bursting at the seams. How did we get this far? Where did I go wrong? Why didn't I make you leave?

How could I allow you to pull the tiny snag on my dress and completely unravel me? How could I allow you to creep inside, plant a bomb…BOOM! Can this be the death of me?

No, it can't be, because now I'm tired, my dreams are on the line, and I want to get away from you. But how do I escape your womb, cut the umbilical cord, and sever all ties that you have glued?

Oh Mistake, don't you know, that I have had enough, and I'm ready for our marriage to end? Don't you think that you have held me hostage, handcuffed, far too long, and this relationship we should suspend?

Dear Mistake, I have something for you, a gift, take it, you deserve it, and NO, there's no objecting.

Take it, it's wrapped all nice and pretty. Open it up and inside you'll find something you're not quite expecting.

It's a bill of divorce that was a long time coming. It's the exact prescription for your disease. I'm tired of telling you, begging you, and pleading with you on my red bloody knees!

Oh Mistake, ALL mistakes, you have to go and leave my life because I am destined for more. I am kicking you out of my beautiful house, and yes I am I slamming and deadbolting the door.

I tried to warn you, but you pushed the line when you tried to conquer me, my marriage, my family, and my finances. No, I'm not listening any longer to your side of the story or the details of the circumstances.

I realize how you simulated a maze full of gray haze that was meant to extinguish me in a dark ball of confusion. But now the dust has settled, all that you have conjured up about me and you is your fantasy, a daydream, an illusion!

I told you once, twice, and I'm now I'm telling you again and again. I'm no longer a slave chained to this toxic, poison-filled relationship, and this lopsided union. Now, it has got to end.

But before you go, let's set the record straight and make a few things crystal clear. I am not you, you are not me, and don't you dare try to pretend you can't hear.

Do you hear me? I said, do you hear me? I am not my mistakes!

Chapter 4

You Are Not Your Mistakes

Early Mistakes

The very first time I scraped my knee roller-skating, I was around eight years old, and the pain I felt was unimaginable. I knew that whatever I did to cause myself to fall and scrape the flesh off my knee was something I never wanted to do again.

When I skated, I did not normally watch out for tiny rocks on the sidewalk and would often skate over them without any problems. But one particular time, a rock got caught in one of the wheels of my skates, which caused one wheel to stop while the other wheels kept rolling. This created a scenario in which one leg hyperextended forward while the other stood still. I lost my balance and scraped my knee on the pavement.

Naturally, I cried and ran inside to my mom. I wanted her comfort, reassurance, and her assistance to get my wound bandaged. The next day, walking was painful, and I had to decide if I was ever going to put on that pair of roller-skates again. I became so afraid of getting hurt; I didn't ever want to think about that level of pain. But after my mother's encouragement, I ultimately decided that skating was fun and worth the risk of getting back out there and trying again. I was already a good skater; I just needed to be more careful. However, this was one of the first times that I became aware of how one mistake could cause fear and try to determine my next decisions.

As a child, it's common to be completely unaware of your environment and the hidden dangers that await you. It's not until you experience deep pain, fear, or rejection that you, too, begin to question your actions to see if did you something wrong.

When I was in fourth grade, I struggled with the steps of long division. It didn't matter how many times I saw my teacher perform the steps on the board, I felt like I couldn't remember how to do them. I remember being taught in school and at home to always ask for help if I didn't understand something clearly. Of course, I raised my hand and explained to my teacher that I didn't understand what was happening.

To my surprise, she scolded me and embarrassed me in front of the entire class. She felt as if I should have already understood and memorized the steps. She acted as if I was wasting her time by asking for help. Soon after she scolded me, I thought, *What did I just do?* I could feel that burning feeling of shame on my face. I could feel others judging me and looking at me as a failure. I asked myself, what could I have possibly done to experience such shame and embarrassment?

I didn't think that I deserved to be treated that way. I thought that it was unfair to be publicly humiliated in front of my peers. Ultimately, those feelings caused me to hate math and myself. I immediately lost confidence in my ability to learn and I lost confidence in the wisdom to ask for help when I needed. I developed a personality trait of never wanting to ask for help. I'd rather figure out something on my own than be publicly humiliated by the "stupidity" of a question.

That one mistake began to shape other areas of my life and lasted a long time…even into adulthood. It took a long time for me to recognize that I could learn and be successful in math. In fact, I took college-level statistics, calculus, and corporate finance. I even took two accounting courses. However, for years I was intimidated by math and by questions that overwhelmed me.

What I learned from that childhood scenario is that mistakes can inflict two types of long-lasting consequences on someone. The first type of consequence is the result of self-inflicted harm that occurs when you make a mistake due to your own naivety, ignorance, or lack of preparation. The second type of consequence is one that stems from you doing something right, but results in a negative outcome or reaction. It's not really a mistake, but it still presents itself as one. The significance and impact of the type of mistake, is not as important as the skills you gain from recovering from them. Learning how to recover from your mistakes quickly puts you on a fast track to learning more about yourself.

Since we know that some mistakes are inevitable, focus not only on avoiding them but also on how to learn from them and recover quickly. Recovering from a mistake requires you to examine your emotional responses and your attitude toward things or people involved in the incident. Every misstep requires healthy recovery. As a someone once said, "Just because it's functional, doesn't mean that it healed the right way." The significance of this is that you don't want to be a "functional mess." It's better to take your time to recover and heal wholly than it is to pretend like you are okay when you really are not.

On the voyage of discovering your identity, you are going to make some mistakes. You might even sink. However, understanding what you did wrong in the past and learning to refocus and live in the present will help you mature faster and develop in your identity. Remember, you are not your mistakes!

What Is a Mistake?

A mistake is an error in action, calculation, opinion, or judgment caused by poor reasoning, carelessness, or insufficient knowledge.[8] A mistake is designed to infiltrate your thinking to make you aware that you have done something wrong. Its purpose is to identify your errors in order for you to correct them, but often, mistakes can be stifling because they promote fear. This could take the form of fear of failure, fear of success, or fear of making another mistake.

---

[8] *Oxford Dictionary*, s.v. "mistake" (accessed on July 25, 2020, from https://www. lexico.com/en/definition/mistake).

Once you make a mistake in a particular area, you are likely to not be as open to diving headfirst into that area again. You may beat yourself up over and over, and even if you try again, you will likely have some hesitation or hidden reservations. Initially this may seem advantageous because your reservations operate like a defense mechanism. However, when a mistake creates habits of fear, it multiplies and develops into an identity of its own with patterns of maladaptive behavior. This will cause you to live your life overly cautious and averse to risk.

This is unhealthy because faith in God requires considerable risks. He took a risk on you by sacrificing His Son's life to give you a better one even though there was no guarantee that you would ever accept Him and this new life He desires for you. We have to be willing to take risks on God as well and trust Him to be exactly who He says He is. When we allow mistakes to shape our wisdom and all our actions, reactions, and decisions, we limit our ability to see clearly into a situation.

Mistakes Are the Breeding Ground of Fear

Second Timothy 1:7 states "God has not given us the spirit of fear, but of power, and of love, and of a sound mind" (KJV). This means that holding on to fear positions us to be powerless, hateful, and unstable in our thinking.

Think about all the times when you were deathly afraid of something. For example, speaking in front of a crowd of peers for the first time, interviewing for your dream position, or getting your first loan to start your business. Many times, if you allow fear to speak for you, your mind and body will resist sound reasoning, God's logic, faith, and clarity in your thinking or, as the Bible calls it, "soundness of mind." Fear is the number-one goal of mistakes and the number-one enemy to faith in God.

Hebrews 11:6 states that without faith, it is impossible to please God. For that reason, living in fear prevents you from accessing true love and having authentic faith. Without authentic faith, you cannot walk in your identity because you will be unable to obey God or please Him. Although God's love for us is unconditional, obedience to God helps to create the necessary pathways that lead us to our fullest purpose. Obedience helps to unlock the gate to understanding your purpose and calling in God.

Because God's love is unconditional, He permits us to think and respond for ourselves without forcing us to love Him genuinely. Although God does not desire to withhold any good things from us, because He is a good Father, He will not give us more than what we are ready for. We cannot allow any mistakes to suck us into spirits of fear and anxiety. They are contrary to us reaching spiritual maturity in our identity-discovery process.

Release and Forgive Yourself

Some mistakes may not be complete blunders but may still have a huge impact on you and your life. These mistakes have a way of making you feel sick, depressed, upset, and angry. Mistakes are often the gateways to depression. They lodge you in self-pity, which may negatively affect your self-esteem. This is why releasing yourself from the guilt of mistakes is an essential component to sound identity development.

Letting go of mistakes requires forgiveness of one's self. It requires you to realize that whether you made an error through poor judgment, poor reasoning, carelessness, insufficient knowledge, or even blatant foolishness, your life is not over. You can decisively press the reset button on life and start over. You may not be able to completely fix or eradicate the effects of the mistake; nevertheless, you can still choose your next steps more carefully and more intuitively. You still have the power to change the trajectory in which you are going.

As mentioned previously, it's important to recover as quickly as possible from mistakes because they affect your growth, potential, and maturity. If you delay in your recuperation, your mistakes can easily keep you fixed in your comfort zone. Although it may feel safe, it is certainly limiting. Functioning from a level of comfort may restrict you from reaching your full potential as your past mistakes serve as an excuse for not trying something new. Hence, the faster that you are able to grasp that your mistakes are an action but are not you, you free yourself to try again, to do something different, something greater, and something more liberating.

Don't allow your mistakes to strangle or suppress your goals and dreams. Don't use your mistakes as a crutch to keep you from moving forward in life. Your most authentic self will thank you later.

Distinguishing between Your Identity and Your Mistakes

Before you can distinguish yourself from the mistakes you have made, it is helpful to examine how your mistakes have affected your life. Acknowledging your mistakes and forgiving yourself will allow you to cleanse your heart and mind from the negative emotions resulting from your errors. You must let go of all regret, shame, sorrow, and disappointment.

These negative emotions, although real, are not conducive to forgiving yourself. It's okay to mourn for a period of time, but ultimately you must let go of your disappointments and actively decide to change the course of your life by renewing your mind (Romans 12:2). When you renew your mind, you are allowing God to transform the way that you think, and you replace your old thoughts with new "God thoughts."

When there are conditions that are out of your control, do not apologize for these factors. Instead, discover the elements that you can control and aggressively begin to move forward. Always take responsibility for your part in a mistake but don't be afraid to acknowledge the factors that were out of your control or situations in which someone else was to partially blame. Forgive them and yourself.

Go through every blunder that has left you feeling sorry and replace those feelings with an optimistic action plan filled with detailed steps focused on reaching new goals. Begin to identify areas in which you can improve and make better decisions. These skills will help to refine your character, strengths, and ability to recover from setbacks, all of which are essential to maturing in identity development.

Feasting on the Word of God, actively praying scriptures and reciting them, will help you learn more about your Father and teach you how to think and become more like Him.

Oops… Here We Are Again!

There are times we make mistakes that are really conscious decisions in the moment but later become mistakes that we look back on with remorse. It's like being on a diet and seeing your favorite food or a piece of cake. You know that cheating will satisfy you in the moment, but you also know that there is a risk that this one act will ultimately set you up for behavior that will ruin your diet. My husband always says that if you give yourself permission to cheat on your diet one day, you are giving yourself permission to cheat at any time. Although some people can survive cheat days, they usually do not endure for long or achieve their weight loss goals.

These same concepts apply to decision-making. Either you are all in or you are all out. Any going back and forth sets you up for failure and defeat. Sometimes we make mistakes that are not necessarily sins or things that are wrong, but they still feel like personal failures. Other times, mistakes can be sin or contrary to God's instructions for our lives. It's important to remember that although God doesn't condone *any* sin, He loves us all unconditionally and grants us grace for repentance and forgiveness.

When you fail in any area of your life, you must release yourself from shame and condemnation because it could create a cycle of depression that will subsequently lead you back to making the same mistake again and again. When you stumble, you must go through a process of self-examination to determine why you failed in the first place. Ask yourself the following questions: Why did you fail? Did you *really* want to succeed or were you trying to please someone else? Do you have excuses ready that you could easily hide behind? Did you have a back door open that made making a mistake or failure easy? Were you fully committed?

Was there an unresolved emotional trigger that led you to lose self-control? Were you giving in to rejection, fear, or the words spoken by another? Did you give in to negative thinking or negative words spoken by you? Were you empowered to succeed? Did you have a plan to be successful? Did you set yourself up for success or failure? Were your motives for being successful coming from a pure place and coming from God, or were they motivated by getting back at someone else, proving yourself to someone else, or pleasing someone else?

Did you fully renew your mind with the Word of God to change your behavior? Never forget that God is ready to forgive anyone who comes to Him with a true, repentant heart. Even if your mistake or failure was not a sin, do not wallow in disappointment. Recover, reset, and move forward quickly if you want to be more consistent and successful the next time around.

Stop and Reflect

The hard work begins... It's time to dig deep.

1. Take the time to release yourself from every mistake that you have ever made. Go all the way to your earliest memory where you made a mistake that caused you pain. (Was it something that happened in your home, elementary school, on the playground, in a friendship, in a secret, in a lie, at your first job, in your first relationship, with your parents, with yourself?) Simply renounce all of your mistakes by saying, "I made a mistake, but I am not my mistake."

2. Pray and ask God to remove any residual effects from the mistakes you made such as fear, pain, unforgiveness of self or others, or a calloused or hardened heart.

3. Write out every self-defeating thought that comes to your mind because of a mistake that you made. Write next to every thought a positive, self-encouraging phrase that you can use instead. If possible, find a supporting scrip-

ture to replace the old thought. This will help you train your thought patterns and renew your mind, as it says in Romans 12:2. This will also serve as an action plan to prevent you from going back to your old way of thinking.

4. Lastly, forgive yourself and write out three things that you need to do that you refused to do before because of a mistake. Then set a deadline for when you are going to complete each of these three items.

5. If you feel like you've never let a mistake hold you back or you are already completely fearless, do three new things that you have never done before that seemed difficult for you to do emotionally or psychologically.

Not Defeated

My plan was as young as a newborn kitten, but today's milk curdled and waxed centuries old.

Although I was young as the sun's early rise, this wasn't the first time I was left alone, desperate, and abandoned out in the cold.

I could feel the powerful wind descending, but the violent tempest I could not perceive.

The tornado I expected, the debris and the wreckage, but the steady creeping flood came to deceive.

I exchanged blows with this storm for so hard and for so long, but against its jaws, I could not win.

I even searched deep, into its hollow mouth, but found no answers, only its cunning grin.

Innocently I slept in the bed of the storm's howl, deceived into thinking its vexation would be quick, a short-lived season.

Yet when I begged for relief from its twisted, razor-sharp teeth, mercilessly it struck again, as if I committed high treason.

The blackened, polluted waters began to drown me and crush me into a finely pressed powder.

Not even my own will could save or defibrillate me or halt this impending onslaughter.

I bellowed, hollered, and screamed as loud as the trumpet in my voice could.

Still, no one was near or heard a tear. My disastrous cacophony rang quiet as an ant scratching wood.

Mauled by the fury and the fangs of the flood surge, I held my breath until I couldn't.

I felt like a woman in agonizing childbirth, ordered not to push, because too soon, she shouldn't.

Yet my last breath seeped out like a pinhole in a balloon, and oxygen seemed to escape me.

I flagged down a friend, a possible lifesaver, but they waved goodbye and betrayed me.

It was at my last moment that I spotted a rope, thrown out to me by a familiar face, I thought.

To my distress it was a net, a noose, a trap, oops…now I'm caught.

But you must know, I needed to survive, and this friendly gateway seemed to be my only sensible option.

I knew I'd been framed, but who else could I blame for tasting the sweet love potion from the cauldron of a bigger concoction?

So I reached for the familiar face trying to escape certain death, but more pain and torture I found.

Love began to whisper, my heart began to wither, and I sunk to a place deep in passion underground.

It was in this underworld that I found myself shackled and trapped in love that covered my wounds.

I was intoxicated in the fantasy and suddenly seduced in the lust of these new love tunes.

But I was bleeding blue in a place where I had to mask, for it was only a mask that could beautify me.

But I wasn't living; I was only existing with love as my secret, covert identity.

This was tricky because the love was real but so was the rejection and the deep hidden pain.

The loneliness, the bitterness, rage, and unforgiveness, what more rancor could I gain?

Was there relief or mysterious peace in a spinning world filled with my sorrow?

Would my search for security in the midst of ambiguity steal my only chance to see tomorrow?

How far could love haul me, tow and pull me, under its shadows, how long could I try to hide?

Where could I find rest, if not in my home-grown nest, where only unpredictable dysfunction could survive?

Although rest seemed out of reach, the sun shone bright and my strength and vitality returned.

When I removed the mask, I was transparent at last, and I evolved with an inner fire burn.

I was no longer a kitten trapped in an adolescent prison but a woman of power, force, and vitality.

I came back with vengeance, temperance, and repentance, and with a vivacious audacity.

Victorious I emerged like the flood that once surged but instead I wore the honor of a fearless conqueror.

Now I could stand with a missile in my hand, wearing the protection of God's love as my full mighty armor.

I didn't have to hide or try to get by, forsaken in this world by myself or alone.

I could breathe at last, and not run so fast, because the wind of this storm had been completely overthrown.

My God came in, just when I thought I couldn't win, and crushed the storm's annihilating power.

He commanded the storm to stop; on the mountain, He placed me on the top, and He rescued me in that very selfsame hour.

Now I have joy, rest, and peace in Him, and strength to fight the storm of another day.

But this time, I have power, dominion, and wisdom, and I can never again let a storm make me a frail castaway.

Defeated I am not, but transformed I am, solidified into a new me, but thickened with brick and mortar.

Defrauded by life, a cadaver I became, but now I'm morphed, crafted, and shaped by the perfect potter.

If you didn't know me before you'd assume that my life's door swung open quick and easy,

But the storm I broke through was not child's play, trust me... it was not that breezy.

I had to learn to shed the layers of scales constructed of hurt, despondency, and depression.

Underneath, a treasure was unearthed full of glamor, beauty, and a virtuous reflection.

If you find yourself fighting a storm, a threatening attack, designed to take you out,

Depend on God; no weapon formed against you shall prosper, trust, He will surely bring you out.

I declare I am not defeated, but transformed I am, fashioned for an era in which I am needed the most.

The battle was never for me to fight, it was to find Him, and power in His Holy Ghost.

Chapter 5

Rise and Reset

Boxing with Life

Life has a way of making you feel like you're in a never-ending boxing match with a powerful storm. Even when you think that the bell will ring, signifying rest, a water break, or the end of a round, more time is added to the clock. It feels like you're in a constant fight, dodging blows and counterpunching every chance you get. Even when the storm is not raging, your expectation for its arrival puts you on edge, makes you tense, and keeps you wondering what could possibly be next. There's barely any time to lick your wounds and figure out where you are bleeding before the next gust dashes in to take you down.

Even the most optimistic people can be caught off guard by a storm. They too may be left wondering if they are ever going to get a break. There are many times in life where you feel that you just need a breather as you grow tired, worn out, exhausted, and fatigued from ongoing battles. This is where the term "battle fatigue" gets its name. Don't forget that life doesn't have to remain static. Even when you think things will never change, do not give up hope. Life can change, your situation can change, and your environment can change.

It is easy to become a prisoner of a powerful storm without knowing how to get out, if there even is a way out. These are the type of storms that make you feel like you are in the fight of your life; you may in fact be fighting for life itself. The important thing to remember about boxing with life is that it is a boxing match. This means that every punch that is directed at you must be answered with a block, a shift in your feet, and multiple counterpunches. In other words, stay in the fight and keep boxing until it's over.

You may not get a knockout each time and you may be left bruised and battered, but as long as you fight strategically, the points can tip the match in your favor. Each time you fall down or lose your balance, get up, take your stance and keep fighting. Enduring the storm will build your strength and stamina and prepare you for larger battles to come. You must rise, you must reset, and you must keep going.

Sometimes we may feel like sheep on the way to the slaughter but we must remember as the apostle Paul said in Romans 8:37, "we are more than conquerors, and gain victory through Jesus Christ who loved us." We were not built to break but to conqueror, to win, and to triumph.

So put on your boxing gloves and square up for the match. Keep fighting. We must remember that the Holy Spirit that dwells on the inside of us is greater than anything we can face in this world. We must also remember Romans 8:28: "We are assured *and* know that, God being a partner in their labor, all things work together *and* are, fitting into a plan, for good to *and* for those who love God and are called according to His design *and* purpose" (AMPC). You are worth God's investment. He wants you to succeed, and His plan is perfect.

To the Victor Goes the Spoil!

It was during a Congressional debate in 1831 that William L. Marcy said, "To the victor belong the spoils."[9] He was referring to the fact that "each time a new administration came into power, thousands of public servants were discharged and members of the victorious

---

[9]   Smokey Stover writing in *The Phrase Finder* (June 18, 2004, accessible on https://www.phrases.org.uk/bulletin_board/32/messages/793.html, last retrieved July 25, 2020).

political party took over their jobs." In Mark 4:27, the Bible says, "No man can enter into a strong man's house, and spoil his goods, except he will first bind the strong man; and then he will spoil his house." This scripture is specifically referring to Satan as the demonic strongman and Jesus as the victor. It is letting us know how to bind the enemy and capture everything in life that God has desired for us.

As children, we never anticipate our adult life to be as tough and as arduous as it often is. We are naturally optimistic and hopeful, and we carry a bright perspective on what life has to offer. Even when our home lives were far from perfect, we expect that once we reach adulthood, things will change because we will have more control over outcomes and our experiences. This is not to say that life is *always* hard, or a struggle. However, when life reveals its sharp fangs and bites us in our most sensitive places, it can really shake us to our core. Just as the phrase goes, "life happens."

This could happen as the death of a close loved one, an accident, a failure, or even depression. When life goes wrong, it is easy to develop an overly cautious mentality that can progress into harmful defense mechanisms. Over time, we can find ourselves spending so much time fighting for life and learning to cope with its disappointments that we essentially forget to fight for our purpose.

You can become so accustomed to fighting that even when there isn't a fight, you find yourself creating one. Everyone has heard of that person who is addicted to drama, who is always fighting or contentious in every situation. It's not always true that they want to live a life full of strife; they have just become so accustomed to fighting and defending themselves that they inadvertently create a fight when there isn't one, out of comfort and a need for security. Fighting becomes their norm.

No one wants to fight an aimless battle, but when you are fighting just for fighting's sake, you miss out on the opportunities to reap the benefits of the trials that you have endured. You can learn a lot about yourself, your values, your character, and ultimately, your identity, after enduring a long battle. Life storms reveal your strengths as well as your weaknesses and provide insight on how to move with better precision. This is why it's important not to only focus on brutal components of the storm but to reach for the gratifying rewards that come at the end.

In Exodus chapter three, when God was preparing His children to leave Egypt, He instructed the women to borrow the finest clothing, gold, and silver jewelry from the Egyptians in order to "spoil" them and to confiscate their wealth. He was teaching them the importance of engaging in battles that are fruitful. So as the long-standing English idiom states, "to the victor goes the spoils," understand that in any battle you win, you should reap all of the benefits, treasure, and rewards from engaging.

You should never enter a battle where there isn't a spoil to be gained. This is why people always say we should choose our battles wisely. Every battle should have a worthwhile outcome. God never intended for us to be in purposeless fights.

It Was a Setup

A war is made up of a series of smaller battles, and each separate battle can determine the trajectory of the entire war. You win some battles easily and others are won by your opponent. Sometimes in order to win the war, you have to do something that seems counterproductive but that will ultimately lead to victory. There are times when God challenges your faith and asks you to do something that on the surface seems like what He is asking will make the situation worse.

In Exodus chapter fourteen, the Lord told Moses to tell the people to go back to Pihahiroth and camp out there, between Migdol and the Red Sea, near Baalzephon. This meant that the Israelites would actually be traveling backward. When Pharaoh received the report about where the Israelites were located, he took his chariots and six hundred of his best men with him and pursued the Israelites, thinking that he would capture them in their weakest state.

When the Israelites saw Pharaoh and his army coming, they became afraid and complained to Moses that they were better off in Egypt serving Pharaoh as slaves than to be consumed by his army in the middle of the desert. They didn't understand why the Lord wanted them to go backward to a place that seemed to put them in a trap.

However, it was a setup. God knew that them going backward would cause Pharaoh to think that the Israelites were lost in the desert, locked in without anywhere to go. In his pride, Pharaoh would think that he could easily pursue them and conquer them. Although the Egyptians did pursue after the Israelites, God had a larger plan. He told Moses to stretch out his rod over the Red Sea. The sea would part so that the Israelites could walk across on dry land with walls of water on both sides. Moses comforted the people by telling them to "stand still and see the salvation of the Lord; the Egyptians that you see today, you will see no more."

After all the Israelites crossed the sea, God told Moses to use his rod again to collapse the walls of water and reunite the Red Sea. However, this time, all of the Egyptians, Pharaoh and his army, would be in the middle and would be destroyed by the water. This particular story demonstrates that sometimes in order to win, a seemingly backward progression is necessary. This act of faith and obedience was a setup for God's glory.

Sometimes when we are engaged in a battle and we have an upset, we think that we have lost, or we are facing defeat. In actuality, God is preparing us to win the war. Do not get discouraged by upsets. It's the perfect time for God to demonstrate that He is ultimately in control. You must trust Him for your victory. Sometimes, we simply have to stand back and see the salvation of the Lord because the battle doesn't belong to us anyway. If we fight by faith, we will often see that what the enemy meant for bad, God will turn around for our good. The enemy is the one that is being set up, not you. Let God get glory from every battle.

After a long season of battle, it's important to refocus and reengage yourself. If you have fallen or faced defeat, you must learn how to rise again and launch a counterattack. Rising again is not about knowing everything about a battle before it happens; it's about arming yourself with appropriate weapons and protection to increase the likelihood of you winning the next one. It is about dusting yourself off after facing defeat. Too often, we sit back and accept defeat instead of dispatching a counteroffensive against the enemy.

Yet, it's difficult to recover from a brutal attack when you don't recognize what led you into the storm, why you were unprepared or underprepared, or why the storm was prolonged. Furthermore, if you developed destructive coping mechanisms to protect yourself from the heartache of the storm, it will make your recovery process more challenging and you will be disabled going into your next battle.

Following a period of perpetual combat, self-examination is necessary to become more knowledgeable about your tender areas. You want to create a strategic plan to lead your counterattack and work on your weaknesses. Some of the signs of poor coping mechanisms that usually result from losing battles are selfishness, rigidity, and deep-seated anger.

For example, in my late teens, I experienced a series of ongoing battles that left me feeling lost, ashamed, and ungrounded. In order to protect myself from the hurt of others, I grew increasingly selfish. I only concerned myself with what was in my best interest, how I was going to be successful, and whether or not something was going to benefit me the most.

This selfishness extended into my young adult life. I did not know how to care for others. I only cared for them as long as their actions benefitted me in the long run. If their actions did not benefit me in some way, I cut them out of my life quickly. I was not concerned with whether or not they needed me, if I may have needed them, what their weaknesses were, or how I could contribute to helping them within our relationship. I did not have any grace for others and did not allow myself to be vulnerable in many relationships.

Although my actions were not blatant (I was kind, nice, and agreeable), deep down inside, I resented many relationships in which people did not understand my pain. This behavior was dysfunctional because I blamed them for hurting a part of me that I never gave them access to in the first place. Consequently, I would not make deep connections with others or establish long-lasting friendships. My own needs outweighed any relationships I was a part of. I had to heal and learn about my weaknesses in order to rise again and face my battles more wisely.

Jab, Cross, Hook

Sometimes in life you feel discouraged because nothing is going as planned. You may have tried everything you possibly can to find answers, seek God, and trust Him but still feel so lost. Every method that you have used in the past no longer works and you feel completely out of options. You remind yourself that everything is working according to God's plan, but you can't seem to figure out what His plan is all about.

This is the hardest part about travailing. To travail means to "engage in painful or laborious effort."[10] It is the process of pushing forward no matter how bad the process hurts. It hurts to not have answers, explanations, or a plan. It tests your faith, your patience, and your resilience. It's painful to watch others move forward while you feel stuck in neutral. But you must keep pushing forward. There is joy on the other side of these birthing pains.

Although you feel that your situation is an emergency, God can see what's on the other side of your pain. He knows how to groom you for your purpose, and He knows how best to process and prepare you. You must trust His process and not rely on your own emotions. He has invested something great in you, and He is expecting a return on His investment.

Do not ignore these birthing pains or dismiss them as unnecessary; without them, your destiny would not come forth. God has formulated you so uniquely that there is nothing you can do to increase the urgency of His response. He will respond to your needs in the way that He sees fit. Although you may be subject to time, He is not. Remain diligent and steadfast and watch how He grows you and nourishes the seeds of endurance you have planted. Your job is to stay in the battle: jab, cross, and hook.

---

[10] *Oxford Dictionary*, s.v. "travail" (accessed August 26, 2020, from https://www.lexico.com/en/definition/travail).

Sidelined and Derailed

There are times in life when something throws you off completely. You might sense it coming, or it can happen without warning, but no matter what, the result is the same.

Maybe you got fired, your spouse cheated on you, you received a frightening diagnosis, or you lost an important friendship. You may spend some time mourning the thing that you have lost and may have set your dreams or goals aside. It's possible that you don't feel like fighting anymore for a while. However, you must recover from this derailment and not allow it to take over your identity process.

After taking some time to reflect, you may realize that you have put some of your dreams on the backburner, you have lost yourself in some relationships, and your identity is not as clear as you previously assumed. You may begin to think about what you should do next. The simple answer is to pivot. Once you realize that the way you have been living is inconsistent with your identity, you must make a conscious decision to shift into a new direction.

Taking these active steps will enable you to change the course of your direction to get your dreams back, identify your passions, and discover your purpose. If you have been complaining, sulking, and whining, now is the time to stop, dust yourself off, and start over. It is time to press the reset button on life. It's never too late to change directions.

What's holding you back from making these necessary changes? What are your fears? Are judging yourself harder than others are judging you? What will your forfeit by choosing to remain the way you are? Do you want to simply exist, or do you want to live boldly, loudly, and on purpose? Do not let a derailment keep you from reaching your final destination.

Get on the Track

To regain your dreams and get back on track, you must begin a process of self-evaluation. You must take the time to examine all the lies that you have told yourself. Have you decided that you are always going to be a certain way? Have you determined that your situation is not currently getting any better and so therefore it **cannot** get any better? Are you too hard on yourself or are you your own worst critic? Are you harder on yourself than any other person in the world?

Even as you did in the reflection phase at the end of chapter 4, begin to reexamine every lie that you have told yourself and replace those lies with positive affirmations. For example, "I'll always be poor" can be changed to "I'll earn more than enough money." Begin to go through every nook and cranny of your life, your personality, your character, your fears, your emotions, your relationships, and your spirituality, and replace every lie that you've allowed to take root with a new statement of truth. Ensure that you are not living perpetually in a defeated mindset. If you think like a defeated person, you will not ever be able to get back on track.

Preparing for the Rematch

The moment that you make the active decision to get off the sideline is the moment the devil comes for a rematch. He knows that you have become "decided" about moving forward and this becomes a prime opportunity to get you to go backward before you really ever got started.

In order to prepare for the rematch, it essential that you examine what the enemy wants to accomplish with his attack. For example, if the enemy is attacking you with sickness, he may be trying to get you to accept the sickness as your own, to doubt God, and to get you to give up on your healing. This could possibly lead to premature death, which may prevent you from accomplishing your purpose on earth.

Or maybe he's attacking your spouse with the goal of causing division and strife in your home. This will bleed over into your children's lives and ultimately stress your faith in God. He may try to destroy your entire family through one incident. It could be a simple argument or disagreement that opens the doors to strife, which leads to division, brokenness, divorce, and, ultimately, he may even try to get you to separate from God Himself.

Once you determine what his agenda is, you can consciously decide to ensure that you are not going to allow what he's trying to accomplish. Next, you must discern the attacks or the weapons that the enemy uses against you. Because he cannot control your future, the only weapons he uses against you are the same ones he used against you in the past. This is particularly important during seasons of distress.

Even if you know that you are stronger than you think you are and know that no weapon formed against you will prosper, you must understand how you are being attacked so that you can respond wisely. In my life, the two main attacks that consistently followed me were rejection and depression. The goal of depression is death. Even as a little girl, I would pray for death because I thought death was my friend and a place of comfort. I thought it was a place that would end my pain and frustrations and provide me relief from the traumas I faced daily. Subsequently, every attack in my life would always lead back to rejection and depression with the ultimate goal of ending my life.

For example, if I struggled with my weight, I would feel low self-esteem, which would lead to depression, which would lead to thoughts of death. If something went wrong in my marriage, I would feel regret, then insecurity, then low self-esteem, then depression, and again death. If I didn't have enough money, I would feel lack, then fear, then rejection, then low self-esteem, then depression, and again death. If I could not find a job, I would feel rejection and discouragement; I would feel like giving up. This would again lead to depression, leading to thoughts of death. If I could not handle criticism, I would feel anger, bitterness, insecurity, and depression again. If I was feeling inconsistent, I would allow my space to get cluttered, which would lead to anxiety, fear, discombobulation, destabilization, emotional insecurity, depression, and then again death. Even when I began to worry about debt, I would go into fear, then anxiety, then regret, then insecurity, and finally depression.

I am intentionally overstating this example to demonstrate that whatever attack you are experiencing, it has a major purpose. Every attack the enemy aims at me is meant to lead me back, no matter what, to feeling rejected and then depressed so that I will not have the will or the desire to live. This has remained consistent throughout my life. Because I know this now, I can position myself to counter the attacks he's bringing my way. I am empowered to never give in to what he's trying to accomplish in my life.

For example, if I'm feeling the burden of debt, instead of going into fear I can encourage myself by declaring scriptures that speak against lack. I can weaponize myself with the Word of God to stand against "every wile of the enemy."

Each person has something that the devil uses against them. This is usually something that's been there your entire life. Although it may take many forms, it's usually the same attack, repackaged differently, to disguise itself. Complete a self-inventory and determine the attacks that the devil uses against you and prepare yourself to stand against it. Even after you have determined what the enemy's agenda and the types of attacks he uses against you, you still have to position your heart to serve the Lord through the attacks and not give up.

Psalms 100:2–3 reminds us to "serve the Lord with gladness: come before his presence with singing. Know ye that the Lord he is God: it is he that hath made us, and not we ourselves; we are his people, and the sheep of his pasture" (KJV). This scripture is a perfect antidote for countering the enemy because it's easy for us to allow our carnal mind to serve the Lord in bitterness, unhappiness, anger, and frustration. However, the scriptures say to serve Him with gladness. It confuses the enemy when you position your heart to be thankful when you could be bitter.

We have to remind ourselves that we didn't create ourselves. This includes our flaws and our shortcomings. Although we are each responsible for self-improvement, God did not make a mistake when He made you. He desired you to be here just the way He designed you. You simply have to renew your mind, obey His word, and position yourself to overcome every test that comes your way.

Understand that you are a son or a daughter of Christ and with that comes privileges. Just as a preacher once said, if the enemy is not chasing you, it may be because you're not doing anything worth chasing. The more you grow in your identity, the harder he will come after you to attack you.

Don't be weary in well-doing. No boxer wins a fight by ignoring the strengths of his opponent. Instead, he studies the opponent's strengths and weaknesses before the fight. Understand that you are the enemy's case study, so he should become yours. Since he spends his time learning your triggers, your weaknesses, and your shortcomings in order to use them against you, study how you can move against him effectively. The Bible instructs us in Second Corinthians 2:11 to not be ignorant of Satan's devices so he can have no advantage over us. You must outbox and outsmart your opponent.

Full Speed Ahead

Once you let go of the expectations of others and decide that you have nothing to hide or fear, characteristics that make up your authentic identity will begin to resurface. You will shed any inauthentic layers for the real you. Then your God-given passions will emerge. Through careful self-reflection and examination, you'll notice what fuels you to live life.

Passion is really a type of hunger that feeds off your purpose. Your gifts can also help you discover your passion. If you find that you are already passionate about many things, it is important to pivot those passions in the right direction. The right direction will be the one that allows you to be who God has created you to be and not a false identity that you have allowed yourself to live within.

To pivot your passions in the right direction, you must seek the root of why you are passionate about certain things. If the root of your passion serves only you, then you may have selfish motives. Selfishness will rob you of your ability to be completely fulfilled in life. Selfishness can cause endless voids of depression and sorrow. If the root of your passion only serves others in a way that drains instead of ignites you, then again, you may have to examine the root of those passions.

Many people serve others in a way that causes them to not care for themselves are really stuck in a people-pleasing trap. They are so concerned about not being accepted that they buy love through service and gifts to others, or other means where they can feel needed, loved, affirmed, or appreciated.

When you discover your identity, you'll find that because you were born and created by God, that alone makes you enough. Your birth alone makes you worth it, valuable, priceless, and deserving of God's love. You do not have to seek validation or approval in the acceptance of others. Your existence proves that you're valuable to God. However, as soon as you decide to disobey God's instructions or begin to live a life contrary to what He has told you, then you devalue your need to exist. Never forget that the purpose of your existence is to bring God glory.

Stop and Reflect

Put your boxing gloves on and open up your journal...

1. Examine what battles you are constantly in, battles that you feel have always existed, reoccur, or never completely go away.
2. Do you believe that it is possible for you to fully release this battle into the hands of God?
3. If so, why haven't you fully released it? Or once you have released it, why do you pick it back up and try to fight it on your own again?
4. If not, how can you increase your faith so that you can fully release the battle?
5. Identify any other aimless battles that you are facing in your life. Examine why they are there (i.e., to exhaust you, waste your time, take advantage of your resources or your kindness, etc.).
6. What situations are you facing, or have faced, that have thrown your life off course? What are you doing currently to regain your focus?
7. Write down three strategies you can use when the enemy tries to throw you off again.

Chapter 6

Matters of the Heart

Heart Posture

On our Christian journey, we frequently need attitude and heart adjustments. Our heart can indicate the maturity or immaturity of our identity development. When unlocking the pieces of your identity, it's easy to respond to God as if He is a man. But we must remember that we interact with Him through the Spirit. If we look at God through the lens of a human being, we may compare Him to the way we interact with others. It is important to make this distinction in order to have the heart of our Father, to accurately scrutinize our heart posture and examine our motives.

Your heart's posture speaks to the way you interact and respond to God. If God asks you to do something, and you do it grudgingly or with a spirit of compliance, then you might as well not do it all. God is not simply seeking compliance from us but a willingness to submit. There is a difference between forced obedience and true surrender.

For example, in the Word of God, we are instructed to love our enemies. An immature approach to this instruction would be to love your enemy only because the Word of God says for you to do so, without seeking to understand why. Without understanding, your love for your enemy will not be pure; it will remain superficial.

One reason God asks us to love our enemies is to teach us how employ His grace and compassion. Grace and compassion are never needed for the innocent. Loving your enemies not only teaches you God's grace and compassion but extends an opportunity for you to express humility and defeat pride. This is because all of us have been guilty of something; in this we were technically an enemy of God and needed His grace, love, and compassion.

If we are empathetic and can realize that we too need God's love, grace, and compassion, we will readily give it to others, even our enemies. Once we understand God's motives and His heart, we can also change our motives and our heart posture will align with God's. We can then move from a spirit of compliance to a spirit of intentional obedience and a heart positioned for pure love. Consequently, we will no longer feel that we love our enemies because God has told us to do so. Instead, we will understand that God loves our enemies and has grace and mercy toward them, and in becoming more like God, we choose to willingly love our enemies as well. Choosing to love our enemies will show the true posture and character of our heart.

Mathew 5:44–46 states,

> But I say unto you, Love your enemies, bless them that curse you, do good to them that hate you, and pray for them which despitefully use you, and persecute you; That ye may be the children of your Father which is in heaven: for he maketh his sun to rise on the evil and on the good, and sendeth rain on the just and on the unjust. For if ye love them which love you, what reward have ye? do not even the publicans the same? (KJV)

This scripture is a perfect reminder that we do not demonstrate true love if we can only love those who love and care about us. Recently, I trusted someone to make some investments on my behalf. I thought that I thoroughly vetted this person, asked all of the necessary questions about their experience, credentials, and reputation.

I waited several weeks before I decided to trust this person to be my broker because I didn't want to make a decision in haste.

Long story short, this person was a professional con artist. They took my initial investment and more. At first I was hurt, angry, and completely distraught over what had happened. I wanted to do things the right way. I wasn't looking to "get rich quick" and I didn't have any unreasonable expectations. Still, I was robbed.

After sobbing and moping for a few days, I decided to send an email to this false broker explaining to him that not only did I forgive him but that I was also going to bless him by sending him more money. Crazy, right? Not exactly! The Bible says in Matthew 6:21, "For where your treasure is, there will your heart be also" (KJV). I had to understand in my heart that this man needed God's grace although he was guilty. In order for me to put my heart in true forgiveness, I wanted to make a declaratory act by faith to put my money where my mouth was. If I know that I do not serve money, or mammon as the Bible calls it, and if I know that I truly forgave that man, it shouldn't be hard for me to sow forgiveness, grace, and mercy into that man's life in the form of money.

I did not do this so that I could get some type of heavenly reward but to make a radial act against my own flesh and emotions. So in this way, I blessed a man who despitefully used me and took advantage of my trust and ignorance. As soon as I sowed into his life, I felt so much peace and relief from the sorrow and anger that I had for him. I wanted to show the enemy that not only did I discern the attack he tried to use against me, I was trained and prepared to counterattack. I know that God is going to take care of me and has given me grace when I didn't deserve it.

God showed me through this pain what it really meant to love my enemies, to bless them who cursed or hurt me, to do good to them who hate me, and to pray for them who despitefully used me. I encourage you, if you are ever facing an issue where you need to demonstrate radical obedience to the Word of God, find a way to do exactly the opposite of what your natural mind tells you to do. The grace and relief you will experience will catapult your faith spiritually.

Motives and Intent

Heart posture is not about *what* you decide to do but rather *why*. It begs the question, "What is incentivizing you to do a particular thing?"[11] Heart posture is important because it reveals why we do everything we do. We can do something right, but if our motives are wrong, technically what we did was wrong as well.

A perfect example of this in the Bible is in Genesis chapter 20, when Abraham told King Abimelech that Sarah was his sister and not his wife. Technically, Sarah was his sister because she was the daughter of his father and not his mother. However, he told a half-truth because Sarah was *truly* his wife as well. What's important is not what was said, but what was *not* said. Abraham used deceit to protect himself and Sarah, which means that he lied by telling a half-truth. Even though his motive was to protect, his motive was also to deceive in order to protect, and therefore it was still wrong, and God caused barrenness to come upon King Abimelech's household.

In John 1:1, we learn that God is His word, and in Hebrews 4:12, we learn that God (through His word) is a discerner of the thoughts and intents of the heart. This means that motives matter to God just as much as the actual actions. Our heart posture must be examined in everything we do. As Christians, we assume that all our motives are usually pure. We think that we are doing things because they are the right things to do and because God has told us to do them. However, in humility, we must examine our decisions through the heart posture of God. We can deceive ourselves into thinking that the motives behind our decisions are always pure, but we cannot deceive God. He knows the underlying intentions that drive our thoughts even before they enter our heart.

When we question why we are motivated to do something, we cannot examine the factors on a surface level. If we do, false reasoning may rule our decision-making and ultimately displease God.

---

[11] Dr. Matthew Stevenson, *Strange Fire: Examining Motives in Ministry and Discerning Offerings of the Heart* (CreateSpace Independent Publishing Platform: 2012) Chapter 2, pp. 17–21.

For example, a person may say that they are working really hard on their job because they want a promotion so that they can earn more money to provide for themselves and their family. However, the true underpinning and depth of their motivations may be to get validation and affirmation, to prove wrong everyone in their past who said that they will never become anything, and to satisfy their mother's or father's nagging words about how they don't earn enough money. On the surface, it may appear that they are undertaking a noble feat, working hard to provide for themselves. But when you dig deeper into their heart, you discover unhealed wounds that reveal the true motivation. Being driven by impure motives will lead to irrational decisions, unhealthy competition, selfish ambition, comparison, and, ultimately, pride.

It is essential to understand that our heart is really our offering to God. This is why we pray to God to create in us a clean heart and to renew a right spirit within us (Psalm 51:10). We must be careful to ensure that what we offer God is coming from a pure place. Even when you want to do the "right" things in the name of God, having the wrong motives makes it the wrong thing.

In First Samuel 10:8–9, Samuel gives Saul specific instructions:

> And thou shalt go down before me to Gilgal;
> and, behold, I will come down unto thee, to offer
> burnt offerings, and to sacrifice sacrifices of peace
> offerings: seven days shalt thou tarry, till I come
> to thee, and shew thee what thou shalt do. And
> it was so, that when he had turned his back to go
> from Samuel, God gave him another heart: and
> all those signs came to pass that day.

Not only did Saul receive specific instructions to wait for Samuel to return but God also transformed Saul's heart. It's important to recognize that in order to obey God, a heart transformation must take place. Even after God renews your mind and heart, it is up to you to remember to obey Him and not follow after what you *think* is right.

In Samuel chapter 13, we see that after Saul waited for seven days for Samuel to return. He grew impatient and decided to offer sacrifices himself. This was a costly mistake that led to him forfeiting his rights to the kingship. Although Saul wanted to do the right thing for God, his impatience, his own will, and his disobedient heart posture led him to do a wrong thing but for what he thought was a good reason. This resulted in a catastrophic outcome. God does not want us to offer Him an impure offering even if we think that we are doing it for noble reasons. If your heart is toxic, anything that you do from that position will turn into an impure offering and will contaminate everything involved.

What you are praying for and what you are praying about will often reveal the motives of your heart. It's important to look at the content of your own prayers. To measure what's going on in your own heart, write down all the things that you have been asking God for and then ask why to each one of those areas. You might ask yourself the following questions: Why am I doing this; why do I desire or crave this; what is inspiring me to keep doing this or asking for this; who or what is this for; what does God think about this, are my motives to satisfy me or God?

Oftentimes, we will discover that there are things that we have not put on the altar of God. We must place our own desires, thoughts, and ways on the altar in order for Him to burn off anything that is not according to His will. Practically, this is a willingness to forgo one's own desires in order to seek God's and follow His plan. It requires us to give up some things that we want in exchange for what God wants for us.

In Isaiah 58:8–9, we learn that God's thoughts and ways are higher than our own, meaning more advanced, developed, sophisticated, superior, important, and more insightful than our own. We must ask ourselves, what have we not offered to God that He wants? What are we offering to God that He does not care about, and why are we offering God what we are offering? When you learn to seek God's heart and not just the hand of His blessings, He will often reveal to you spiritual strategies, insight, and answers to questions you have been asking for years.

Seek God for who He is; meditate on Him and His word and not just on the blessings that He has promised you. This will help cultivate and realign your motives.

Attitude Adjustment

Frequently, it is our own attitude that gets in the way of us hearing God, having clarity, receiving His instructions, and understanding our identity. Our attitude is a key indicator of our ability to understand who we are. It reflects our innermost thoughts, beliefs, and patterns of behavior in response to what we think about ourselves.

Although it is difficult, we must learn to see ourselves the way God see us. Second Corinthians 4:7 says, "We have this treasure from God, but we are only like clay jars that hold the treasure. This is to show that the amazing power we have is from God, not from us" (ERV). God sees us as treasure in an earthen or earthly vessel. This means that He looks beyond what is easily seen from the outside and trusts that the Spirit that He has put inside of us is more valuable than the faults, mistakes, and brokenness seen from the outside.

Ephesians 2:10 reminds us that we are God's workmanship and His handiwork. His word tells us that "it is He that has made us and not we ourselves." Because God knows the end of our life as well as the beginning, He can look at all the facts presented to Him about us and still make the decision to love and favor us, nonetheless. He knows that there is treasure inside of us even though we may appear to be simply clay vessels.

It is easy to get locked into a detrimental mindset that surrounds us with a self-defeating attitude, low expectations, comparison to others, and fear. God sees us as sons and daughters, heirs to His kingdom and a part of his royal priesthood. He even goes as far as to say that "He will remember our sins no more and they will be as far as the east is from the west" (Psalm 103:12). It is only our adversary the devil and we ourselves who persistently and habitually bring up the past as a way to disqualify us from our future.

We must change our attitude and renew our minds to see ourselves differently. This will require us to ask daily, "What does God say about me? What does God think about me?" When the report of the enemy is presented, and even if our own thoughts betray us, we must make ask ourselves, whose report will we believe? We have to actively declare that we will believe the report of the Lord, which states who we are and not who we were or what we did.

A Matter of Doubt

Where does doubt come from? Doubt is the response to disappointment, and disappointment stems from not getting what you have asked for or from having expectations that are not realized. Not getting what we want is not permission for us to retreat in doubt or disappointment. Rather, it is an opportunity for us to respond in humility and reverence; trusting that God's love will protect us from ourselves. Disappointment should warrant praise and thanksgiving because we know that His Word is true, and that God wouldn't withhold anything good thing from us as long as we walk uprightly and according to His righteousness (Psalm 84:11).

When we are left disappointed, we often become frustrated, temperamental, and stymied in our spiritual growth. However, we really need to refocus by using disappointment to discover breaches in our faith. A matter of doubt is really a faith issue. Every disappointment that we face should prompt us to seek God more deeply, more intently, and should encourage us to patiently await His answer and instructions.

Next, we must ask ourselves, what is the purpose of faith? Because we know that Hebrews 11:6 reminds us that "without faith it is impossible to please God," we know that one purpose of faith is to please God and to bring Him glory. Faith urges us to expand beyond our own wisdom in pursuit of the supernatural intelligence of God. Faith should be our human response to God when we face disappointment.

We must grasp that if God gave us everything we wanted every time we wanted it, we would not likely seek Him harder for the things He wants us to learn and know. All of these lessons are critical to us properly managing our destiny and are crucial to us building an intimate relationship with Him. Disappointment should draw us closer to seeking Him and not further away, sinking in doubt.

God is tired of us behaving like spoiled children, taking every "yes," every gift, and every blessing for granted. There is an expectation from God that at some point we should be able to teach others how to respond to God in faith. We should know how to understand and proceed when we are disappointed by our current circumstances. We should not allow doubt to push us away from God. Hebrews 5:11–14 says,

> We have many things to tell you about this. But it is hard to explain because you have stopped trying to understand. You have had enough time that by now you should be teachers. But you need someone to teach you again the first lessons of God's teaching. You still need the teaching that is like milk. You are not ready for solid food. Anyone who lives on milk is still a baby and is not able to understand much about living right. But solid food is for people who have grown up. From their experience they have learned to see the difference between good and evil. (ERV)

When we are disappointed, uncertain, and lack clarity, we often cry, sink into doubt and fear, and have angry tantrums like children. We should wonder how God feels about such tantrums. When a two-year-old child has a tantrum because you didn't give him exactly what he wanted when he wanted it, there's an expectation that at some point, he will understand that he cannot have everything he wants because it doesn't benefit him. However, if a ten-year-old child has a tantrum after you've taught him this lesson, you're likely going to question his maturity and his ability to cope with decisions.

So imagine how God feels when we respond to disappointment with doubt, anger, or fear after we have sought Him about a particular thing. He expects us to be mature and to respond by seeking Him more intently until we have received an answer. We should continue to reapply our faith, trusting that He knows best.

Understanding God through disappointment makes our victories more valuable and more treasured. As one of my best friends said to me, "We always want God to put a rush order on the things we want but we sure don't rush into the things God wants us to do." We don't rush into our callings, we don't rush into obedience, and we don't rush into studying the Word of God. Often, we cower and say that we want more confirmations or a prophetic word or a sign before we move into anything God says.

One thing to remember is when things do not align in the way we think they should, we should not *always* interpret the misalignment as God telling us "no." He could be easily teaching us patience or waiting for the right moment to bring something to pass. If not careful, our disappointments can lead us into unnecessary fear and doubt that blocks our ability to have a correct heart posture toward God.

Later, I will discuss in more detail how to pray and seek God in order to actually get answers from Him. Most of our disappointments come from not knowing how to pray and seek God properly. This is because "God can't answer a prayer He's never heard."[12] But, more on this in chapter 8.

Who Is God to You?

How you approach God is very telling of both your identity and your heart posture. It reveals how you think about yourself and how you feel God thinks about you. It is effortless and easy for us to declare that God is good without really understanding His goodness.

I know that we think that His goodness is simply wrapped up in what He did for us, what He kept us from, and how He helps us through life's trials. However, it is a common and universal habit for us to approach God like we approach our natural father, mother, leaders, teachers, or authority figures.

---

[12] R. Watson Jr., "Foundations Class, Part 4: Faith" (July 1, 2019).

For example, if your father was abusive, unloving, or despondent, you might approach God as if He is an abusive, unloving, and despondent father. If your Father was absent and didn't really care about you, you may know that God cares, but you may behave as if He doesn't. This is because you are interacting with Him based on your perception of your natural father. You might filter every trial that you experience through that particular lens. If you felt that the authority figures in your life ignored you, didn't give you enough attention, or abandoned you, then you might approach God like He's forsaken you.

In the time that I have been alive, I have felt forsaken, abandoned, and not defended. I have felt like I was stepped on when I was down, abused, inadequate, and not accepted for who I was. I lived in fear of being punished or chastised and I was made to feel like I was worth "less." I was publicly humiliated and embarrassed and felt forced into obedience and submission. I experienced rigidity, inflexibility, cruelty, hateful behavior, and extreme cynicism.

If I approached God through the lens of my experience with other authority figures, whether they were parents, teachers, leaders, family or friends, I would interact with God like He is one of those figures. I would pray to God and then believe that He would forsake me, despite me knowing clearly that His Word says He would never do that. I would feel like He was punishing me every time something went wrong when clearly in His Word He tells me that there is grace extended to me and even mercy for my mistakes.

I would feel like He didn't really like me or wouldn't accept what I had to offer, which is silly because He's the one who made me in the first place. However, when you don't know who you are or are uncomfortable with who you are, you will be confused about the way God speaks to you, leads you, guides you, and loves you. You will inadvertently approach Him like you approach others.

So ask yourself, how do you approach God? Do you know what His Word says about you? Challenge yourself to write down several scriptures that speak to how He thinks about you and how He cares for you. If we view God through the eyes of our natural father or mother, this could lead to us having expectations from God that is outside of His character.

God is not like a natural parent in the sense that He doesn't think or operate in the way we think He should. I have heard many times that some people decided to become atheists because God let them down. They think that He should have done something for them when they wanted it and how they wanted it. However, if we could command God to do whatever we wanted whenever we wanted, would that make Him God, or would that make us God? God is sovereign, but He also expects us to embrace Him as a father. He is ready to extend grace and unconditional love to those who come to Him.

An Unyielded Heart = A Heart of Rebellion

An unyielded heart reveals who and what is really in control of a person's soul. A heart that is unyielded is one that cannot submit and is ultimately a heart that is rebellious. It is a heart that is governed by emotions such as fear and panic. It is ruled by personal feelings and personal perspectives that block objectivity, clarity, sensitivity, awareness, bravery, and courage. It is one that is a full of pride, a prisoner to personal preferences, a slave to stubbornness, and a hostage to idolatry.

You cannot grow without trust, commitment, and submission. First Samuel 15:23 states, "For rebellion *is as* the sin of witchcraft, and stubbornness *is as* iniquity and idolatry" (KJV, original italics). Since the goal of witchcraft is to control or to impose one's will on another, this means that the goal of rebellion is to deny the sovereignty of God, to resist His authority, and to exercise personal control by living according to one's own rulership. This scripture also points to stubbornness being as idolatry because to be stubborn is to worship one's own ideals, preferences, and opinions.

However, Jeremiah 17:9 says, "The heart *is* deceitful above all *things,* and desperately wicked; Who can know it?" (KJV, original italics). This lets us know that we cannot always trust our own hearts, feelings, and emotions because our own hearts can and will deceive us. Have you ever heard the phrase "follow your heart"? This is often dangerous because our hearts can be deceived by our emotions, immaturity, and lack of wisdom and clarity. Many people expect others to know the depths of their heart when they don't always know it themselves.

I'm sure many can find an example where they thought that their heart told them something, only to learn that they had been deceived by their own wishes. Only God and His Word, being made flesh, knows and judges the thoughts and the intents of the heart (Hebrews 4:12). Therefore, a rebellious heart will remain in a perpetual identity crisis, always panting, and running, a vagabond, never finding a resting place or an identity to call home.

Although submission is required by God, learning to submit can be a difficult process because many of us experience a great deal of pain and disappointment in life when we are not in control. No one usually starts off rebellious but when submitting doesn't get one the desired results, rebellion often seems easier.

As a young girl and even in the beginning of my teens, I did my best to submit to my mother's authority. In her efforts as a single mom to protect me, she often proved to be controlling, inflexible, rigid, and overbearing. Although she worked hard to protect me and to give me what she thought was best, as I got older, I felt limited in my personality expression, my career choices, love choices, friendships, and experiences. While I submitted to her ideals for most of my adolescence and teenage years, that submission brought me to a place of feeling emotionally clogged and bogged down because I was suppressing my true feelings and wasn't submitting to her willfully.

Although I cannot blame her for my emotional response to her parenting style, I felt as if I could not be who I really was, which brought me to a place of depression and misery. This was not merely my mother's fault but my reality nonetheless. My submission was forced, and I often felt that her expectations and standards seemed unbearable.

My response to living this way for an extended period of time, like many teens, was rebellion. I felt like I was living in a pressure cooker and eventually blew the lid right off. Once I started down this road, it was difficult to get realigned again because I was in a war with myself. I was torn between what my mother wanted for me, what I wanted for myself, and what God wanted and expected of me. This was a recipe for disaster because I could not decide who was *really* in control.

To compound my issues with rebellion, I also felt deep rejection from mother wounds, father wounds, and my peers. When I was growing up, I wished that my father had fought my mother harder to be in my life and I wished that he fought harder to develop a trusting relationship with me. Although he often asked me if I wanted to live with him, I wished later on that he had fought harder to convince me of his love. I also felt that my sister's father, whom I loved and was much closer to, also did not fight hard enough to stay in my life after he and my mother separated. It seemed that everyone caved in to my mother's wishes, included me.

Even worse, I experienced a great deal of rejection and teasing from male peers growing up and I funneled all of this rejection into my self-esteem or lack thereof. As a consequence of feeling rejected, I rejected others because it's easier to reject someone before they can reject you. After I got married, I projected all my male-rejection issues, compiled with my mother and father wounds, onto every man, boss, leader, pastor, mentor, or authority figure, including my husband. I was afraid to submit to my husband or to anyone because I thought that submission would bring me pain.

Not only could I not submit, I also could not fully commit to anything that I thought would limit my choices, my freedom, my goals, personality, or my overall well-being. In sum, I was unyielded, unsubmitted, rebellious, and unable to commit. This seems strange since I was already married and had many covenant relationships. However, I was ignorant about the state of my heart posture for many years. It was not until later that I learned it was my unyielded heart that was affecting my spiritual growth, my ability to trust my pastor, and my ability to commit to anything within my church or in my personal life that I thought threatened my liberties. I truly developed a heart of rebellion.

Although I knew that God *wanted* me to submit, I did not understand that God **required** my submission. God was not asking for forced obedience; He was asking for a willing heart to submit. He knows that rebellion is a covenant-breaking spirit, one that will destroy relationships, friendships, partnerships, marriages, and even oneself. Eventually, it will pervert our ability to follow and therefore our ability to lead. As someone once said, "Every great leader was once a great follower, and every great teacher was once a great pupil."

Submission is the process of willingly giving your power to the hands of another and trusting them to lead you to your next level of growth. In reality, submission is trusting God Himself or trusting God to use another person to lead you. If you cannot submit, you really cannot trust anyone, and therefore you can never firmly commit to anything. If you can't trust anyone, you won't have the ability to trust God and you won't have the ability to commit to *His* plan for your life.

Although submission is challenging and can cause personal pain and disappointment, and stretch you outside of your comfort zone, it is still required by God. Without learning to submit, God cannot deal with your heart posture effectively because you will not listen, obey, or live in godly discipline. Often when you are being led, you feel that you know what's best for you better than the person leading you. However, it's not about what you can see or what you think you can see, it's about allowing yourself to be led and allowing God to direct your path instead of you choosing it for yourself.

Submission builds character, integrity, patience, meekness, and love. Once I finally learned how to submit and have a yielded heart, one that did not do whatever it wanted, I learned to yield to God. It was then that I began to grow spiritually. If you cannot yield to the person sitting in front of you, you definitely cannot yield to God whom you never seen.

When I was first learning to submit, I did it bitterly and resentfully because I was full of pride. I had to learn that I could not submit in my own strength. It took renewing my mind and godly discipline and grace to learn how to submit and commit. I had to learn not to lean to my own understanding but to submit to the will and understanding of God.

Obedience

A simple definition of obedience is "compliance with an order, request, law or submission to another's authority."[13] Yet when you obey God, it is more than just an act of compliance and submission. You are often required to give up your comfort, your preferences, and what you think is "right." It is easy to submit to something or someone when you regard them as excellent, competent, and of superior value or quality. But what if God asks you to submit to something that you think is subpar or foolish?

For example, just as Jesus says in Matthew 5:43–46 that it's easy to love your friend or those who love you but much harder to love your enemy, could obedience follow the same structure? Should I willingly obey someone whom I feel doesn't deserve my submission? If loving your enemy exemplifies the true love of Christ, who loved us beyond our faults, then true love is demonstrated when we love the seemingly unlovable.

Could the same principles hold true with honor? It's easy to give honor when it is due an honorable person. However, can we honor someone when they don't deserve it? Can we honor an absent father or mother? Many children today do not honor their parents because they were never shown how to honor. As a parent, I take time to tell my children that I thank and honor them for being obedient, and I thank and honor them simply for being my child. You may ask why. Well, it's simply because I want to set the precedent for honor in my household.

There are many who believe that you shouldn't reward or honor someone for doing what they are "supposed" to do because they are expected to do what they are doing anyway. My response to that is "That's man's wisdom!" We know that man's wisdom is foolishness to

---

13 *Oxford Dictionary*, s.v. "obedience" (retrieved August 27, 2020, from https://www.lexico.com/definition/obedience).

God because in His Word we learn that because God "is not mocked, whatsoever a man sows, that he shall also reap" (Galatians 6:7–8). If you want to reap things of the Spirt, meaning things of God, you have to demonstrate sowing into the "right things" that will produce a favorable harvest. Therefore, if I would like to reap honor as a parent, I must first sow it into the very ground from which I want to reap it, meaning my children.

There may be times when I as a fallible parent may make mistakes and not deserve honor, but my children will know how to honor me anyway. Again, obedience is similar in structure because it requires us to lay down our will in order to honor God.

Since obedience is a form of submission, we have to examine our willingness to acquiesce our will. Can we submit to an incompetent boss? Can we submit to someone whom we feel knows less than us? It's always easy to obey when what we must submit to matches the level of authority we believe is fitting. What if God deliberately requests for you to submit to someone or permits for you to be in a situation in which you know, and He knows, is substandard to teach you how to examine your level of "true" obedience? You have not demonstrated true obedience until you can obey or submit to someone who isn't easy to submit to.

Why would God call you to obey someone you deem fit or excellent if you can't obey someone smaller? If you don't learn obedience as a discipline at all levels, you will not be able to submit when God calls you to a higher level of obedience. You will likely dishonor the person or structure that God brings to you. God doesn't wait until you have received what you want before He trains you on how to submit. Rather, He instills His principles and character in you along the way.

In Exodus, when Miriam and Aaron began to murmur and complain against Moses stating, "He's just a man like us...we can lead ourselves," God responded by telling them that they had to follow Him, through clouds, signs, and wonders, while He spoke to Moses face-to-face. He basically asked them, who did they think they were? When walking in obedience to God, we must remember that His wisdom far exceeds our thoughts and logic. Our preferences can lead us into rebellion and become idolatry, which I will discuss later in this chapter. Walking in obedience fortifies your heart posture in contentedness and decisiveness about your future and what God has designed for you.

What Do You Forfeit by Remaining Small?

I once had a conversation with someone much older than me who I respect, and he told me that he was glad that God didn't give him a lot of money because having to struggle kept him humble over the years. My first thought was that he was hardly walking in humility at all. In fact, he was living his life under the deception of false humility.

True humility is not keeping yourself from something in order to prove or justify how humble you are; it is remaining humble with or without any particular thing. For example, a person may say that they refuse to wear expensive shoes because it would make them prideful. It is not the shoes itself that creates pride; rather it is the pride within the person that manifests into a monster of pride because of their heart posture and way of thinking.

We must be careful not to allow false humility to hide within our character. Likewise, there are people who intentionally go out of their way to be unseen. They believe that intentionally taking a back seat or a lower position when they are qualified to do more is them showing humility. In fact, they are demonstrating the exact opposite. Now some would argue that the parable at the wedding in Luke 14:10 speaks about taking a lower seat, but this demonstration is not done to be *seen as* "humble." It is specifically referring to not taking a place of honor when you have been invited by a guest because you feel that you deserve it.

Notice the difference in heart posture; one can demonstrate pride by taking the high seat out of entitlement or one can intentionally go out their way to be *seen as* humble by avoiding the high seat in false humility. Any time a person tries to do something to prove or show that they are humble, they are likely demonstrating false humility. True humility comes from the heart, and the actions of a humble person will be a by-product of their heart posture. It doesn't work the other way around, where a person does something to "be humble."

This is not to say that there are not times when humility causes us to take a step down or a lower seat. I'm instead referring to those who go out of their way to appear humble by stepping down but not because they actually *are* humble. I've also met people with good intentions who did not know they were walking in false humility. For example, they may have been called to publicly minister, pastor, or serve in a broad capacity but they have decided that in order to remain humble, they will simply serve in a simpler capacity in their local church. Although all those who serve the church are valuable, I am speaking specifically to those who have been called to do more but do not because they think that refusing makes them humble.

Again, Jesus acknowledges that those who serve hold the highest honor in the kingdom of God, and there's absolutely nothing wrong with serving in general. In fact, I think most people should be willing to do anything in their local church. Again, I'm explicitly referring to those who intentionally desire to be unseen because they erroneously believe that their actions are out of humility.

Actually, the most prideful people boast about how humble they are, how much they serve others, and how much they give to others. They believe that they are "bragging on God" when in fact they may be deceived by their own heart; they are simply finding creative ways to talk more about themselves. This is not to say that we shouldn't "boast in the Lord" or tell of our testimonies or blessings. This is simply an urge to check your heart posture to ensure you are not walking in false humility.

What's even more important to consider is if you are intentionally remaining small because you are trying to be humble. You must ask yourself, what are you forfeiting by remaining small or by not walking in *all* that God has called you to do? Are you forfeiting your purpose, your destiny, your blessings, your truest and most authentic identity? Many people choose to stay small because they do not want to have to stretch or grow outside their comfort zone. They also don't want the level of accountability that comes with growth. Instead of growing in their identity and moving into their purpose, they will hide under a false sense of humility and forfeit everything God wants for them.

You must also ask yourself, where is false humility hiding? Often, it is hiding in our desires to be humble, in our intentions, heart posture, and our efforts to appear pious. God is concerned about the true posture of our heart; it's written in His Word that He hates all forms of pride.

Never be afraid to become greater because of fear or because of the criticism from your enemies. Never allow the potential attacks from Satan to stagnate your growth. Examine your thinking and activate your faith to believe that anything is possible. God desires for you to live to your fullest potential, anticipating miracles and unprecedented blessings.

Surrendering: Releasing Grip and Control

In order to obey, we must learn how to surrender and release our grip and control. Sometimes, we just have to let go! People who struggle with submission often operate with a Jezebel spirit.

There's a wonderful book written by Ryan LeStrange that goes into detail about this spirit titled *Hell's Toxic Trio*. This is a spirit that is not gender specific that operates on the power of control and witchcraft. As I mentioned previously, witchcraft is simply imposing your will on someone else through methods of control, manipulation, emotional abuse, and guilt; it is imposing illegal authority by usurping power or using word curses and witchcraft prayers. We should never pray that God will force someone to do something that we want because that creates an imposition of our will and not His.

God's design has always been founded upon giving people a choice to make decisions. Their decisions will determine their future and their relationship with God. God loves people who reject Him every day; if He didn't, neither you nor I would have the opportunity to have salvation today.

God has a habit of looking beyond faults and seeing the needs of a person, whereas many of us focus on the outward appearance and what we want for someone. God never sees us merely in our current state. Rather, He sees the drug dealer as a future preacher, the liar as a pastor, and the sinner as a future Christian teacher. As I mentioned before, He finds the treasure in the "earthen vessel," meaning, He sees what we will become.

Surrendering your ability to control something means that you must be free from all fear. Fear is both an issue of sonship and an issue of the heart because if you are living in your complete identity, you will have received the perfect love of Christ, which eliminates fear. If you struggle with giving up your control, you likely are manifesting a controlling personality rooted in fear.

Often, the root of developing a controlling personality stems from a person feeling helpless, rejected, unloved, unsafe, abused, betrayed, disappointed, and powerless at some point or many points in their life. These feelings develop into unbearably deep pain, trauma, and ultimately fear. In order to avoid feeling so powerless, a person may resort to becoming controlling and incredibly rigid in order to feel stable, secure, loved, protected, and grounded. They will exercise their power to control any person or any situation at every opportunity.

Controlling people are the most risk-adverse and fearful people you will ever meet. Their faith remains limited because one cannot operate in deep levels of faith while being tormented by fear. They have permitted fear to rule and resist allowing someone else to lead and be in control; even God himself, because they cannot predict or determine a definite or favorable outcome. These people often catastrophize situations and think in extremes; everything must be absolutely perfect, or everything will go terribly wrong. It's either "my way or the highway."

Perfectionism and low self-esteem are also characteristics of people with controlling personalities. They are easily embarrassed and do not have a sound mind or stable emotions. This definitely described my old personality, but since God did not give us a spirit of fear but love and of a sound mind (2 Timothy 1:7), I had to become free from the pain through which I inherited fears that in turn made me want to control situations.

Anyone who operates with a dominating and controlling spirit cannot think or operate without fear. They have poor emotional intelligence and lack self-awareness. They frequently do not notice how their behavior pushes people away, ruins relationships, or becomes unbearable to those around them. Often, controlling people have difficulty showing love without conditions, are usually indecisive, and lack clarity, focus, and discipline. They often procrastinate out of fear of getting started or fear of not finishing. They struggle to love deeply and truly because of their fears of getting hurt. They can only demonstrate love, patience, meekness, and kindness when they get "their way" or when their conditions are met. If at any point you do something that makes them feel rejected, embarrassed, or unloved, they will attack you, attempt to emotionally manipulate you, make you feel guilty about something, and ultimately withdraw their demonstration of love for you.

The whole point of recognizing controlling spirits is to root out fear and allow yourself to trust God. If there is an area where you find yourself being controlling or emotionally manipulative, ask yourself if there is fear and pain at the root. God wants us free from fear, anxiety, panic, and control.

Hidden Poses

The heart is literally the "beat" of the body, pun intended. It is such an essential organ that it is encapsulated by our rib structure to protect it from injury. Without it, we cannot fully live. Although all of this is obvious to us, what's not always obvious is how our spiritual hearts operate, what hides or poses behind our heart, and how our heart posture determines our spiritual growth and maturity.

First Thessalonians 5:23 helps us define the three dimensions of man as "spirit, soul, and body." This is important to know because mankind is a spirit-being. If you have been born again, then your spirit is alive; but if you have not been born again, then your spirit-man is dead to God and separated from Him. We have a spirit, we have a soul, and we live inside a body. The soul refers to your "mind, will, and emotions."

When you accepted salvation and became a born-again believer, God did not save your soul or your body. Your soul doesn't get saved until the Word of God comes in and changes you, according to James 1:21. This scripture explains to us that it is only the engrafted or the implanted Word of God that has the power to save our souls.

You may then ask, what does a saved soul look like? It looks like a person with "(1) a renewed mind, (2) a submitted will, and (3) stabilized emotions." It is with this understanding that we know that spiritually, our hearts determine the heartbeat of our souls. It is through the heart that the mind, will, and emotions emanate. To understand one's heart is to understand one's motives. Motives matter to God and determine our level of spiritual access, growth, and spiritual maturity.

To pose means to "assume a posture or attitude, typically for artistic purposes or to affect an attitude or character, usually to deceive or impress."[14] Posing is the "fake it till you make it" mentality. It is the idea that one must represent themselves as one way in order to appear as something they are not, or in order to be perceived at a level that one has not authentically achieved. It's common to want to project an image in order to protect our feelings or mask who we really are. No one enjoys being misunderstood, talked about, judged, or even criticized for who they are or are not.

Posing is important to consider when examining heart posture because every hidden pose is a threat to the integrity of the heart. The root verb of the word *posture* is "to pose." God is concerned with our heart posture, meaning the integrity, authenticity, and motives of our heart. Although He expects us to present our bodies as a living sacrifice, according to Romans 12:1, He is not simply concerned with how we appear to present ourselves but the actual intents, thoughts, and our will that resides within our hearts. Our posture indicates the expression of what we may think, feel, and determines how we act or react.

---

[14] *Oxford Dictionary*, s.v. "pose" (retrieved August 28, 2020, from https://www.lexico.com/en/definition/pose).

A hidden pose can take the form of a mask, self-deception, or a wound that lies within the heart. It remains hidden under fear, rejection, and low self-esteem. However, hidden poses are dangerous to our souls. This is because the "Word of God must filter through your soul" (mind, will, and emotions) in order to be effective and help you change into what God wants you to be.

A mask serves as a cover to pose or present ourselves as better off than what we are or in a fashion in which others perceive us in a way favorable or pleasing to us. Many posers feel forced to suppress their real feelings, emotions, and personality in order to "fit in," maintain the status quo, or protect their perceived reputation. Some choose to hide what they really feel in order to please others because they want acceptance, validation, and affirmation. Others fear being judged or misinterpreted.

Since people do not want to be vulnerable, they choose to hide behind their poses. On the other hand, someone may create a false sense of identity in order to keep people out, keep them at an arm's length, or limit who is allowed in. You make think that you know them but deep down inside, they feel unknown because they never permit anyone to get close enough to know the *real* them.

Often when God calls you into deeper levels of relationship with Him, you must forgo your perceived reputation in order to take on His character, His expectations, and His plan for your life. This cannot occur if we are too busy working to protect an image that we created for ourselves and that He never ordained.

Have you ever heard someone complain that no one really knows the "real me"? The truth is these people are posers. They are presenting themselves in such a way to prevent people from knowing them. Ultimately, they do not want to be known. They like the idea of being a mystery to others. As a consequence, they force others to figure them out because they feel rejected and feel safer in isolation. Occasionally, people are tricked into believing that their false presentation or pose is real because they have behaved a certain way for so long. Their bad posture has shaped their character and infiltrated their identity. Any identity not rooted and grounded in Christ is a false identity. True identity comes from understanding one's role in sonship. I will focus more on sonship in chapter 10.

Someone with poor physical posture can be easily spotted slouching and slumping. Poor physical posture can lead to neck tension, pain in the hips, joints, and even feet. Over time, a person can become so comfortable in a slouched position that their spine will take on the curvature of their slump permanently. It can affect the way they breathe, walk, sit, and stand. Imagine how much damage poor spiritual posture can create within our spirit and in our hearts.

Poor heart posture can cause us to lie to ourselves. Since our heart posture is a manifestation of our daily attitudes and thoughts, self-deception occurs in the heart when we hide how we really feel and suppress who we really are. It doesn't matter if this is done to "fit" the expectations that we have created for ourselves or, to "fit in" with the expectations of the culture around us. This main issue with the "fake it to you make it mentality" is a person's heart posture. If you can't be authentic, transparent, and vulnerable with other people, you ultimately cannot be honest with yourself.

We must ask ourselves, what are we really trying to hide and why? What fear is residing in our hearts that we would prefer to hide instead of allowing people in? If you can't let anyone in, if you have deep trust issues, then can you really trust God? Does God have your heart, or do you have it? When we let go of the sense of false identity that we've created to protect our image, God can come in and heal those broken areas so that we can learn who we really are in Him.

I've heard people say, "Well, I do this because I don't want anyone to think ____," or "I do this so that people don't assume ___ about me." This sort of thinking reveals that a person may be projecting a false image or false representation to protect themselves from being judged. We can get so raveled and twisted up in protecting, defending, and defining ourselves that God is no longer our defense or refuge. We become our own defense.

We have to learn to not care what people think about us and realize that we don't have to prove our identity to people. This is not a license to sin but to be authentic. As I mentioned previously, Jeremiah 17:9 reminds us that "the heart is deceitful above all things."

This is literally warning you that your own heart can deceive you and trick you into believing and seeing things in a way that is false. Although character and integrity are always measured, remind yourself that you have nothing to prove when it comes to your personality, financial status, marital status, parenting status, or even your perceived identity. Simply learn to become authentic and be yourself. You will always have those who will reject you, but those meant to be in your life will remain and will appreciate and enjoy the "real you."

Only when we are honest with ourselves can God be truly honest with us and help us identify our true calling, identity, and purpose. He doesn't want us to mask how we really feel. He would rather we be authentic and obtain true change and deliverance. True deliverance occurs by allowing the Word and power of God to get from our spirit and inner man, filter through our soul, and then manifest in our bodies and natural life.

Again, it is only the implanted Word of God that can save our soul, or in other words, change our mind, will, and our emotions. However, hidden poses such as identity masks, soul wounds, bitterness, unforgiveness, hatred, anger, envy, and strife can prevent the Word of God from being implanted. This is why we must unclog our heart and rid ourselves from any blockage that may prevent the Word of God from taking root.

We must remember that according to 2 Peter 1:1–3, God has given us everything we need in order to walk out this life. So if we allow God's spirit to lead us, we will walk in liberty because where His spirit resides, rules, and governs, there is liberty. In fact, it is so refreshing and liberating to be authentic.

Imagine saying no to an invitation that you don't want to accept, wearing something that you really like without fearing criticism, or choosing a career path that doesn't align with someone else's expectations. Imagine making choices without fear from others. Although God-given liberty is not permission to live according to our fleshly desires, it is freedom to walk according to His Word in a way that lets you be "you"!

A preacher once said that God wants unity, not uniformity. What this means is that each of us is colorfully created to be authentic, unique, and different, that we should never aim to be exactly like anyone else. We should aim to bring all of our differences together in the body and work together in a spirit of unity but not necessarily sameness.

Stop and Reflect

Open your heart and your journal. It's time to be honest with yourself.

1. In what ways or areas could you adjust your attitude?
2. Examine why you want the things that you crave in your life. (Everything including losing weight, being fit, your career choice, your decision to be a stay-at-home parent, family lifestyle choices, desires, ambitions, parenting style, education goals, etc.). What is *truly* motivating your goals? Is it acceptance, family approval, a desired to be needed, loved?
3. Identify any disappointments and check to see if they have affected your faith in any way. How can you reestablish your faith in an area of disappointment? Write down at least three ways in which you can begin to trust God again in those specific areas.
4. Identify who God is to you. Are you looking at Him through the relationships you had with your mother, father, leaders, teachers, or other authority figures? If so, how can you begin to truly see God as *He* is and not as one of those figures?
5. What have you forfeited because of the way you think about yourself or because of how others have viewed or defined you? What would you do if these opinions no longer mattered to you?
6. Is there any part of yourself where you pose or mask who you are or how you feel? If so, why? What can you do to become more authentically you?
7. How can you get over the fears of what others think about you and how *you* think about you?

Chapter 7

Clogged

What Is the Blockage?

The first thing that needs to be done by anyone focused on uncovering their identity, is to unclog, by identifying the blockage and its common symptoms. Blockage refers to those things in your life that make you feel clogged, bogged down, sluggish, confused, and disoriented. It's the dead weight, the negativity, the momentum-killing words, influences, and life pollution that keeps you from operating in a healthy way.

There is no point of doing all the work on your "heart posture" if your arteries are clogged. After you reach a place of heart purity, you may need to address the residue that led to your heart trouble to begin with. You must ask yourself what *is* blocking you or *can* block you from discovering your true identity? This is not an exhaustive list, but it can be a person, a community of people, bad memories, unforgiveness, offense, comparison, fear, procrastination, rejection, or a lack of transparency. It can be anything that connects to your heart. These are the areas where you may need professional counseling, therapy, and deep self-reflection.

Symptom 1: Chest Pain!

One barrier that impedes a person from finding their true identity is unforgiveness. Unforgiveness is a type of clog that triggers a person to focus on the wrongs of others. It promotes emphasis on what someone else did to you instead of what you could be doing for yourself.

Frequently, when a person harbors unforgiveness, they will spend most of their time attempting to get others to hear their pain. They often retell painful experiences to others, seek perpetual sympathy, and are often still left feeling unheard. They remain in a constant state of reliving their painful experiences instead of moving forward. Unforgiveness is truly pain rehearsal. You must stop practicing something that you do not want to manifest in your life. Why rehearse pain? You cannot truly focus on your own identity when you are focused on the character flaws in another person. You must release that person of the pain that they caused you and begin to reset and refocus on getting to the core of your own issues and identity crisis.

Furthermore, you must recover quickly. There's nothing worse than a person who spends their entire life recalling bad memories and looking for a pity party because they are determined to get everyone in the world to recognize how someone else wronged them. There is no need to sulk for your entire life, wasting opportunities, squandering time, throwing away your youth or vitality, or delaying your identity development. As I heard a preacher say before, "Are you going to complain until you die?" You must mature past these deep-rooted emotions and press into what is really important.

Symptom 2: High Blood Pressure

Another obstruction that blocks a person from discovering their identity is fear and procrastination. Just like high blood pressure, these serve as silent killers to identity development. They can exist without you ever thinking that they are real and serious.

I believe that fear and procrastination directly correlate with each other and often work in tandem together. This is because many people who procrastinate do so because they have underlying fears and insecurities about failure. They get so worried about not completing something or finishing something that they fail to start. Others delay beginning a project or something new because of lazy habits or because they feel that the pressure of meeting a deadline will make them work faster and better. However, working under pressure for extended periods of time can cause a person to get burned out and destroy their ability to endure long seasons of testing.

Laziness is similar to procrastination and can also be an indication of fear and anxiety. Laziness is defined as having the ability to do something but lacking the motivation to do it.[15] Lazy people often are so overwhelmed by what they feel is necessary to complete that they give up on trying. Lazy habits create a pattern of procrastination rooted in fear. Simply starting something new can trigger feelings of panic and anxiety. Procrastinators often listen to negative self-talk about their abilities and their potential to complete something.

The dangerous factor about procrastination is that it robs you of the opportunity to fail quickly and to learn from your mistakes. This can stunt your growth. A part of life is learning, making mistakes, and, sometimes, failing. The faster you make these mistakes, the faster you can recover and explore what you're made of through them. There is nothing more powerful than the power of a mistake showing you how strong or how weak you are emotionally, physically, and psychologically. Mistakes reveal what's in your core personality, your flaws, where you need to improve, and how quickly you can or cannot recover from a setback.

Although the goal is never failure, failure has a way of highlighting problem areas to work on. It's crucial to use these incidents to your benefit. A person who truly wants to discover their purpose must eliminate lazy habits, procrastination, and must learn to live with godly discipline.

It is hard work to retrain the way you go about starting and completing projects. Nevertheless, gaining these tools will systematically discipline you to seek God more fervently for your purpose

---

[15] *Oxford Dictionary*, s.v. "lazy" (retrieved August 28, 2020, from https://www.lexico.com/en/definition/lazy).

and identity in Him. A lazy person will not have the endurance, tolerance, patience, and motivation to seek God for their true identity.

Diagnosis 1: The Arterial Plaque Called Rejection

Rejection is a huge impediment to discovering your authentic identity and creates one of the largest blockages. It is a plaque that binds to self-esteem and builds up to cause the most issues related to identity. This is because rejection is a two-part entity; one part being the act of rejection and the other part being the response of the recipient of rejection.

The first part, the act of rejection, is the process of someone or some group excluding you intentionally or unintentionally by ignoring you, disregarding you, prohibiting you from having access, or preventing you from some type of inclusion. It is the process of being kept out or left out.

The second part, receiving rejection, is the emotional response that you have after being rejected. Once you are rejected by the act, you may respond by feeling left out, unwanted, undesirable, unwelcomed, uninvited, unnecessary, useless, discarded, and snubbed. This type of response from the act of rejection indicates your level of emotional maturity. This is because you can be rejected (the act) without accepting the rejection (the response). In other words, you do not have to respond like a rejected person.

For example, you may interview for a job and be rejected as a candidate because the employer decided that someone else was a better fit. This does not inherently mean that you were not a good fit, but maybe not the best fit. Responding like a rejected person will mean that you are believing the assumption, that you were not good enough, that you were unwanted, unwelcomed, or undesirable, when in fact, all these explanations may be false. The truth is, they may have rejected you because you did not interview well or because someone else was a better fit. Their rejection of you should not cause you to question your abilities.

You don't have to respond like a "reject" if someone or some group rejects you. Thus, you can be rejected without responding like a "reject." If you do, your response clearly demonstrates that you may have rejection and self-esteem issues.

A person who lives with rejection will always respond as a victim. They will become pessimistic and feel that no one will accept them or that their "truest self" is unwelcome. You must realize that no matter how many times you are rejected, it does not make you a "reject." God has designed you the way He intends for you to be. However, this is not a license to fail to grow, develop, or change. Rather, it is the culmination of understanding who you are, and how to interact with other people well, despite your feelings.

Rejected people generally do not have solid relationship skills or the ability to make sound decisions, especially when those decisions directly involve other people. They have poor interpersonal skills and will react to situations personally instead of objectively. Even if they do act or react, it is usually in a defensive way. Because they always feel unloved and disregarded, rejected people are willing to go out of their way to defend their behavior or their stance on something.

They often remain in their comfort zones to protect themselves from further rejection. They are inclined to be narcissistic and are overly critical of others. Typically, they will reject a person before that person can reject them. For example, they will assume that someone is unlikely to like them or to accept them for whatever reason and therefore will conjure up an opinion about that person in order to reject them, stay away from them, or keep them at a distance. This is to protect themselves from being rejected by that person in the future. It would take more risk and more work for them to get to know a person for who they are, than to easily form a snap opinion about them, and then, reject them.

Rejected people often say things like "they don't like me" or "I don't like their cliques" or "they think that they're better than me." Even if these observations have some truth, a rejected person must examine themselves to see if their behavior contributed to their rejection. Often, rejected people have rejected themselves, excluded themselves, and unwelcomed themselves before anyone else could. Or they may have made a mistake or said the wrong thing and catastrophized the situation, instead of learning to acknowledge their mistake and move forward, building the relationships they are a part of.

It is common for rejected people to have low self-esteem and yet be full of pride. Often, the people with the lowest self-esteem have the greatest amount of pride. Their low self-esteem is in response to learning that they are not really as important as they think they are. They want to feel more special than they are, and when this does not happen, the result is low self-esteem.

Some people are groomed in rejection through methods such as bullying, intimidation, oppression, harassment, and mistreatment. These individuals develop a rejected personality and have allowed their pain to become a part of their identity. These people experience rejection more often because they welcome rejection into their lives. Because they fear that rejection will always be their norm, they unintentionally or intentionally push people away, reject true friendships, reject authentic love, and live a life being rejected and rejecting others. They need liberation from rejection. They need to be released from the mark of living a rejected life through deliverance.

This is the definition of having a stronghold. Their pattern of thinking is maladaptive, and they have an innate unwillingness to change. The lens in which they view life remains one of rejection. It will not matter what changes around them if they do not change the way they view themselves and the way they view others. A rejected person must learn that they are not a reject and that they are accepted, wanted, needed, valuable, chosen, loved, attractive, special, desired, and admitted. They must release themselves of negative thought patterns that speak the opposite of acceptance.

Even if they have not yet discovered the people they should be around or the relationships that are meant for them, even if they have not yet found the opportunities that are meant for them or where they are wanted, they do not have to be rejected. Living rejected will obscure the identity in which God designed you to live within. A rejected person will develop an identity in response to rejection instead of as a result of their purpose.

Other Symptoms: Restricted Blood Flow

Being authentic and transparent is one of the vital ways to learn who you are in Christ because it requires honesty. Lack of transparency obstructs your ability to be genuine and to flow in and with Christ.

Many people claim that they dislike "fake" people but many of those same individuals do not live in a transparent way. Transparency allows you to be open, free, and expressive about how you really feel. It's really about disarming the enemy. If you release your hidden fears, sins, or past, the enemy cannot use it as fuel against you. Transparency allows you to take the power away from secrecy by exposing yourself.

When discussing being transparent, some people may assume that this gives you permission to be rude to others or be critical about them. Transparency should not become a "keeping it real" situation gone wrong. This is because transparency is not about others; it's about you. It's not about being rude or inconsiderate but rather learning to allow "you" to be present without fear of rejection. This does not give you permission to intentionally hurt others in a selfish way, but sometimes when you are transparent, it exposes others that are connected to you. You must carefully consider what is important to release and discern when it is healthy or appropriate before you release any information that could potentially harm others.

In no way does this mean that you should keep secrets that are harmful, illegal, or dangerous to oneself or to others. When in doubt, seek counsel and know that even if you receive some backlash, it is essential for you to be free to flow as yourself in Christ. It is essential for you to feel free to move forward in your life.

Unclogging: Soul Wounds

In First Thessalonians 5:23, the Bible identifies the three dimensions of mankind as spirit, soul, and body. This is important to understand because mankind is a spirit-being that has a body and a soul. It is not until you are born again spiritually that your spirit comes alive. If you have not been born again, your spirit is dead to God and separated from Him. This means that you will be unable to understand the ways, thoughts, and mind of God with human logic.

It's equally important to understand the definition of one's soul. The soul refers to "your mind, your will, and your emotions."[16] As mentioned in James 1:21, it is only when the engrafted or "implanted" Word of God comes into a person that their soul can be saved. We are to receive the Word of God with meekness, meaning with a submissive attitude, with patience, long-suffering, and forbearance. This means that a saved soul is defined as "a renewed mind, a submitted will, and stabilized emotions."

Without getting too deep into theology, God lives in your spirit, and Satan can occupy your soul in the form of your mind, will, and emotions. Without the Word of God renewing your mind, your soul can be tormented. This means you can experience torment in your mind, in your will, and in your emotions. Soul wounds specifically refer to the damaged parts of you that you have never dealt with. These wounds often appear in your life once you begin to make changes to improve your walk with God.

Soul wounds are those deep-seated areas in your life that guide the way you think and operate. Most of them come from areas occupied by deep-seated rejection or your inability to control a situation. When your soul is wounded, you will continue to make choices from a wounded perspective. You may even be outright mad at God. You may feel like everything that went wrong in your life is His fault because He permitted it. This brings me to another central topic to address: God's will.

A great book that sheds more light on God's will is *The Will of God* by Leslie D. Weatherhead. In the book, Weatherhead describes God's will in three categories: "His intentional will, His circumstantial will, and His ultimate will."[17] It's important to understand the "wills" of God. Things can occur in our lives due to God's permissive will, His intended will, and His perfect will.

---

[16] R. Watson Jr., "Foundations Class, Part 4: Faith" (2019).

[17] Leslie D. Weatherhead, *The Will of God* (Nashville, TN: Abingdon, 1972).

Because God gave mankind free will, there are choices that each of us make daily. These choices can be good, bad, or indifferent. Any time we make a choice, and something happens, we cannot assume that it happened because it was God's will for our lives. What I mean is, the results of our choices could have simply been in God's permissive will but not His intended or perfect will.

God's intended will is everything that He has designed for your life. You can be in agreement or out of alignment with God's intended will. If you are out of agreement with God's intended will, then what He wants for your life will not necessarily come to pass because your free will can override His intentions for you. For example, God may want you to be a gifted international worship leader, but you may choose a life of drugs, partying, and self-indulgence. This does not mean that God cannot bring your life into agreement with His intended will, but as long as you continue to override His intended will, then through His permissive will you will continue to live the life you have always been living.

God's perfect will is when His intended will and permissive ensue simultaneously. So in our example, if God intended for you to be an international worship leader, and you answered that particular call on your life, took advantage of the opportunities to sing and become and international worship leader, and you actually become one, you would then be in God's perfect will. This is because what He wanted for you and what you chose to do were in perfect alignment.

There are many people who are violently angry with God for things they believe were a part of His intended will. However, some things God did not intend, but He permits them to happen because He has, in His infinite wisdom, decided to give us all free will. What we can be certain of is that fact that "we know that all things work together for good to those who love God, to those who are the called according to *His* **purpose**," according to Romans 8:28. This is true no matter what "will" things are occurring under.

The reason why we must understand God's will is that knowing when we are out of alignment, and knowing what He intends, can help us manage the damage that soul wounds cause. It helps identify the root of soul wounds, face them, and then heal from them. It also helps us understand the value in learning how to search the scriptures to determine how God speaks and what His intended and perfect will is on a matter.

Personally, I experienced many situations that caused deep souls wounds for me, such as being forced to leave my mother's house six weeks after my high school graduation, losing an apartment once I was married, being mocked and rejected by people who I thought who loved me, being told that I looked like a man, being treated as less than, and countless other situations. I'm sure my life is not an anomaly; many of us have experienced similar situations. Although unique to each individual, each situation still has the power to contribute to the formation of soul wounds.

What transpired during my life is that, once I was rejected and wounded in a particular area, I developed a thought-pattern about that area, that seemed to always guide my future decisions. For example, after losing an apartment, I thought that it would be hard or nearly impossible to get another one, especially a *nice* one. However, once my mind, will, and spirit was healed, I was able to see that nothing was impossible with God. I was able to understand that all people wouldn't reject me and that I was worth loving.

The problem with soul wounds is that they are not obvious. You make think that you are "okay," "just fine," when there really could be some areas of your life where you do not operate from a place of peace. In Romans 14:17, Paul reminds us that the Kingdom of God is not meat and drink but righteousness, peace, and joy in the Holy Spirit. He is reminding us here that if there is an area in our lives where we do not have peace, God's gift of righteousness, and joy, then we are not operating under God's kingdom.

I have met many people who struggle with anxiety. Anxiety is simply fear of the unknown. If God did not give us a "spirit" of fear but power, love, and a sound, mind, anyone allowing anxiety to dictate their life choices are not operating under God's kingdom but are being ruled by Satan's.

People live with things that God never intended them to live with. If you deal with soul wounds, areas that have caused anxiety to rule in your life, and understand how God wants you to live, you can be free. Healing soul wounds requires identifying every area and place in your heart where you experienced deep pain and rejection, and then taking active steps to forgive people or situations that caused you harm. Finally, it requires renewing your mind by discovering how God *desires* for you to live and operate in every area of your life.

Cleaning Out Insecurities

An insecurity is "uncertainty or anxiety about oneself; lack of confidence; the state of being open to danger or [a] threat; [and a] lack of protection."[18] Many insecurities are a manifestation of fear and a product of not receiving the perfect love of God. These types of fears create anxiety, that produces unnecessary urgency, and negative feelings about time.

The majority of insecurities stem from low self-esteem. Low self-esteem is an emotional response to feelings of rejection, external trauma, difficult life experiences, and poor coping skills. Low self-esteem often develops in early adolescence after a child experiences something difficult and or traumatic.[19] However, a traumatic event may not be an isolated occurrence but an ongoing experience with repeated traumatic occurrences. When children feel neglected and are left to fend for themselves, are left alone too much, ignored, or not a priority in their parents' lives, they can often develop a negative self-image. Parent-child relationships are often one of the most common sources of low self-confidence.

Children consistently need to be reassured, asserted, and affirmed. If parents work long hours or make the eldest child responsible for other siblings, or if parents have many children and cannot adequately give each their attention, these children can end up feeling like their needs are ignored and may feel unwanted or unimport-

---

18 Oxford Dictionary, s.v. "insecurity" (retrieved August 28, 2020, from https://www.lexico.com/en/definition/insecurity).

19 Leon Chaudhari, "Self-Esteem Masterclass: Learn to Love Yourself," *Udemy* (accessed May 20, 2020 from https://www.udemy.com/course/self-esteem-masterclass-learn-to-love-yourself/learn/lecture/7740302#overview).

ant. Of course, there are many other situations that can contribute to poor child-parent relationships, but the premise remains the same.

If a person lacks a healthy relationship with their parents, feelings of low self-worth are likely. These individuals will likely look for opportunities to always care for others while neglecting themselves. They can easily turn into people-pleasers or create a disposition that they are open to be abused, neglected, and or mistreated.

Sometimes, a person can have a relatively positive childhood and still have low self-esteem because they have experienced repeated failures, difficult relationships, loss, divorce, long-term illness, chronic pain, or verbal, sexual, or physical abuse. If these feelings are not examined and treated through therapy, counseling, or in other emotionally healthy ways, a person will likely develop low self-confidence that will continue into their adulthood.

Mental health plays a significant role in unclogging the things that block your identity formation. If you are unable to see yourself in a positive way, you will definitely reject any ideas that God has about you if they do not align with your negative thinking. You will reject opportunities for growth, love, and personal development and remain stuck and bogged down by your feelings of self-rejection. Your mental health will govern how you interact with others, affect your ability to build positive relationships, limit how quickly you bounce back from failures, and will decide how you approach your relationship with God. If you are not emotionally healthy, you will live your life with a "spirit of an orphan" because God will constantly have to prove to you that He loves you, that you are enough, that His plans are perfect for you, and that you are worth the sacrifice He made to call you His own. If you can heal past this point, you will be able to clearly walk in the authority and God-given identity that has always been yours. Without this clarity, you will be unable to fully commit to surrendering your will to God's purpose for you.

It's important to mention that becoming mentally healthy takes self-accountability and self-awareness. No one can force you to deal with your problems. Although God will help you, you have to be committed to your own mental health. This will likely lead you down the road to forgiveness. You will have to forgive what you think is unforgiveable. This includes forgiving those who rejected you, and forgiving yourself.

Frequently, people have an expectation that closure in these areas of pain will look like what they want them to look like. This can be an unrealistic expectation. The people who hurt you may never change their behavior, notice the damage they caused, or feel remorseful about their contribution to your pain. They may be struggling deeply with their own mental pain, damage, wounds, and profound hurt. It is not your responsibility to fix them but to deal with yourself.

Closure may look like redefining your relationships with those who hurt you. This does not mean that you will necessarily have to end those relationships, but you may have to change the way you engage with them. It may require that you set appropriate boundaries to protect your mental health. Once you are stronger, you can redefine these boundaries to suit your new mental well-being.

Once you get the emotional healing and closure that you need, others may not recognize that you've changed, or they may not accept who you are becoming. These are called side battles. The more healed you become, the easier it will be for you to recognize these side battles. I call them weapons of mass distraction. The goal of side battles are to consume your focus, your energy, your commitment, and your discipline levels. These battles waste time, energy and resources. They can drag you into carnal and fleshly situations where you no longer operate or respond from the Spirit of God. They will pull you into responding from a place of pain, carnality, and defense.

However, do not expend energy on trying to prove to other people what you are or what you are not because of their inability to see you correctly. Understand how God sees you and pursue your identity in Him as a son or daughter. Keep your peace and continue to make necessary steps to guard your emotional health. Do not get dragged into battles that are not your own or that ask you to compromise your mental health journey. Stay the course and get healed.

Ask yourself, what are you insecure about and what do those insecurities produce in your life? If you are insecure about your body, ask yourself why. Is it because you feel that because your body is imperfect, you will not be accepted or that you will be judged or disliked? If you are insecure about your career, ask yourself why. Figure out what negative thoughts are produced from this. Are you insecure about your age, goals, spiritual maturity?

Discover those areas in your life and address why you feel insecure about those things. Determine if they are producing fear, anxiety, low self-esteem, or any work of Satan. Anything that exists to depress you, steal your joy, peace, happiness, and self-worth is not from God and should be addressed.

People-Pleasing

People-pleasing is when "a person has an emotional need to please others often at the expense of their own needs or desires. This often occurs when a child grew up with an emotionally unavailable parent and unconsciously picks up the pattern of being a people-pleaser in order to engage the despondent parent."[20]

People-pleasing individuals are often incredibly caring, crave social interactions, and aim to make others happy. They will often aim to make people laugh, feel loved, accepted, and cared for. People who aim to always please others at the expense of their own needs usually have issues valuing themselves. They think that if they spend any time caring for themselves that they are being selfish. They have low self-worth and lack confidence to assert their own needs. They do not quickly see or recognize their value, and many times, they can become a doormat for others to walk all over.

Sometimes, these people are the easiest people to talk to and are great intensive listeners. They attract abusers, bad friendships, and bad relationships and become a dump for others to drop off all of their problems. They end up carrying false burdens and weights that are not their own. They will often serve others without recognizing when they are being used, abused, and or manipulated.

---

[20] *Merriam Webster Online Dictionary*, s.v. "people pleaser" (retrieved July 14, 2020, from https://www.merriam-webster.com/dictionary/people pleasing).

This is not a normal godly servant attitude but a "silent passivity and a conflict-avoidance"[21] approach to life. They often can get lost in busyness instead of having a directed focus. They volunteer for the most difficult tasks in order to feel needed, appreciated, and valued. They will serve in a capacity that they have outgrown out of fear and wanting to be accepted. These individuals will give away all of their money, go out of their way to prove their love, and even compromise their integrity to make others happy. They may even develop a habit of lying because they do not want to disappoint someone they care about. They feel urged to compete for the attention of others, have a need to be seen, and constantly seek approval. Still they end up feeling inadequate, small, deficient, and worthless.

The reason why people-pleasing individuals lack a strong identity is because they never have an opportunity to focus on who they really are, what they need, and what is missing in their lives. Because these individuals have an eager appetite to feel loved, they crave acceptance, affirmation, and validation. This results in them living perpetually in an "orphan" state of mind. They never fully accept that they are sons or daughters of God.

People pleasers fail to realize that the type of unconditional acceptance and love that they desperately want only comes from God Himself. Only God will accept them, love them, and show them their worth in Him to the fullest level desirable. He's the only one who can prove to them that they are worth being in existence.

People pleasers also have an inability to finish what they start. They begin projects and give up on them prematurely because they suffer from abandonment issues. It's easier for them to quit and give up on something than to tunnel through. Since they have experienced abandonment, they make a habit of subconsciously avoiding or running from difficult situations. These issues become repeated cycles, preventing them from achieving their goals.

---

[21] Meghan Fritz, "Know Your Worth: Dating Dysfunction," *Town&Gown*, a State College and Penn State e-zine (June 29, 2018, retrieved July 14, 2020, from http://www.statecollege.com/news/Letter-to-the-Editor/know-your-worth-dating-dysfunction,1477024/).

It is God's desire for everyone to understand that when you are born again, you become one with Him. First Corinthians 6:17 tell us, "But whoever is united with the Lord is one with him in spirit" (NIV). It is in this oneness that you discover the full acceptance of God and your complete identity with Him. If you are primarily focused on pleasing others, you cannot possibly focus on pleasing God. Galatians 1:10 states,

> Am I now trying to win the approval of human beings, or of God? Or am I trying to please people? If I were still trying to please peo-ple, I would not be a servant of Christ. (NIV)

This scripture is letting us know that people-pleasing is a form of idolatry. This is because it requires you to actively choose to please "man," the wishes of mere mortals, out of fear of their opinion instead of our omniscient God. You are valuing the opinions of oth-ers over what God has called you to do. It's impossible to walk freely in your identity when you value what others think more than what God desires for your life.

Remember, God says in Exodus 20:3, "You shall have no other gods before me" (NIV). God does not want anything to become an idol in our lives. We must learn to develop a focus on what He desires instead of giving in to people-pleasing to satisfy our needs to feel loved and accepted. The more you learn about who you are in Christ, the more you will realize how much He loves, accepts, affirms, and validates you. You will not have to prove yourself wor-thy. He has already deemed your worthiness by His justification of your sins on the cross. He's already declared His promises for you and for your life. He has already made up His mind about you. He's not working to figure it out. He loves you more than any mere mortal ever could.

Flushing Out the Bad and In with the New
Framing New Thoughts for a Renewed Mind

How do your thoughts clog your mind, your identity, and determine your will? No matter who you are, there are toxic things in your body that need to be flushed out. Our waste systems were created exactly for this purpose.

Flushing out bad waste, through sweat, urine, or solid matter, helps to keep our cell function high and prevents us from getting sick. Without the removal of toxic waste, buildup of toxins could instantly kill us.[22] In our spiritual walk, we need to flush out the bad and regenerate ourselves with a renewed mind. This occurs through examination and transformation of our thoughts.

Our thoughts are the heartbeat and fuel of all of our actions. As it says in Proverbs 4:23, "Guard your heart above all else, for it determines the course of your life" (NLT). This scripture indicates to us that our thoughts shape our actions and determine what we will and will not do. Often, our thoughts reveal whether we have negative or positive thought patterns. They divulge what's in our mind and what is navigating our souls. More importantly, our thoughts often determine what we will speak. Since the way we use our words can determine whether we speak life or death to something, as indicated in Proverbs 18:21, we must carefully examine our thought life. Words have so much power that we must watch what we think and say.

Many people have negative thought patterns because we have not yet renewed their minds in an area. Even if our thought patterns are not negative by our self-determination, they may still be negative thought patterns in the eyes of God. He determines what is and what is not acceptable.

Negative thought patterns can be defined as "a pessimistic outlook on most or all aspects of life" and "believing in a distorted reality that things can't or won't get better." Negative thought patterns can

---

[22] Harwood, Wilkin, Kraus, et al., "Excretory System," *cK–12* (published June 01, 2020, retrieved July 15, 2020, from https://www.ck12.org/biology/excretory-system/lesson/Excretion-MS-LS/).

also be defined as anything we think or anything that lives in our imagination, reasoning, and logic that proudly goes against God's infinite wisdom and knowledge. These thoughts often lead to disobedience, idolatry, and pride.

Second Corinthians 10:5 states "[Inasmuch as we] refute arguments and theories and reasonings and every proud and lofty thing that sets itself up against the [true] knowledge of God; and we lead every thought and purpose away captive into the obedience of Christ (the Messiah, the Anointed One)"(AMPC). Identifying negative thought patterns is one of the first steps we need to take in order to renew our minds.

We must see these thoughts as toxic blockage to perceiving ourselves in our rightful identity in Christ and purpose in God. These thoughts will not only keep us in a false identity, they can block us from hearing God's voice and obeying what He has instructed us to do. In fact, these thoughts can keep us from living within our godly inheritance and beneath the privilege that He offers all His sons and daughters.

Negative thought patterns usually fall into several common categories such as black-and-white thinking, overgeneralizations, dysfunctional worrying, unreasonable expectations, emotional instability, catastrophizing, jumping to conclusions, and playing the blame game.

Black-and-white thinking is the process of reasoning in "extremes." These are the type of thought patterns that say it has to be "this way" or "that way" and there is no compromise or gray area in reasoning. Although black-and-white thinking is useful when you need to choose between two options, it's usually a bad belief system when applied to life lessons and relationships. Thought processes should be rational, discerning, and objective when possible.

Overgeneralizations is the process of "drawing conclusions based on little data, facts, or reasoning." This type of thinking is unrealistic and prematurely makes judgments that can be harmful and detrimental.

Dysfunctional worrying can be defined as unrealistic anxiety that stems from depressive thoughts. This sort of thinking can be described as linear where a person feels that "this one thing definitely causes this other thing" without rational judgment or proof. This sort of thinking causes incessant worry based off destructive reasoning.

Emotional instability is defined as "rapid, often exaggerated changes in mood, where strong emotions or feelings (uncontrollable laughing or crying, or heightened irritability or temper) occur. These emotions are often the result of unhealthy thinking patterns where the emotional outburst is not in proportion to the situation or environment."[23]

Catastrophizing is similar to black-and-white thinking in that it operates in extremes, except catastrophizing always includes a negative emotional response. Catastrophizing is "when someone assumes that the worst will [always] happen."[24] They often have an exaggerated view of the difficulties they are facing. For example, catastrophizing is saying, "Since I'm bad at math, I will fail college. If I fail college, I won't have a great career because I won't be able to get a job. If I am unable to get a job, then I will be homeless or forced to live in my father's basement." Although this example is silly, many people who catastrophize do not realize how extreme their negative thinking is and how detrimental it is for making sound, comprehensive decisions.

Jumping to conclusions is making premature judgments about the outcome of something. It is the process of not allowing time to consider facts and changes in information, and being unable to identify one's own bias.

The blame game is defined as "a situation in which one party blames others for something bad or unfortunate rather than attempting to seek a solution."[25] This is a negative thought pattern that is

---

[23] "Emotional instability: description, causes and risk factors," *Medigoo* (2013, retrieved July 15, 2020, from https://www.medigoo.com/articles/emotional-instability/).

[24] Sian Ferguson, "Catastrophizing?: What You Need to Know to Stop Worrying," *Healthline* (Feb. 02, 2019, retrieved July 15, 2020, from https://www.healthline.com/health/anxiety/catastrophizing).

[25] *Oxford Dictionary*, s.v. "blame game" (retrieved July 17, 2020, from https://www.lexico.com/definition/blame_game).

fueled by deflecting from the facts and avoiding all responsibility for actions. A person who always seeks to blame others will often see themselves as the victim and cannot objectively make decisions clearly or become responsible for their part in a situation.

Negative thought patterns are also thoughts that lead to deception, lying, and incongruence with God's will. Jeremiah 17:9–10 states,

> The human heart is the most deceitful of all things, and desperately wicked. Who really knows how bad it is? But I, the Lord, search all hearts and examine secret motives. I give all people their due rewards, according to what their actions deserve. (NLT)

In this scripture, the heart is referring to the deep parts of the mind and will. It's letting us know that our own hearts and mind can deceive us. As I stated before, this is why we should not always "follow our hearts" but ask God to lead us by His will. Following our own hearts can escort us into the enemy's trickery.

This scripture also informs us that God examines the intents of the heart. This really means that He not only examines what you say and do, He also examines what you think. Sometimes things can come to our thought life that we did not intend to think. These thoughts can be "enemy thoughts" that come directly from Satan. As James 4:7 says, "Submit yourselves, then, to God. Resist the devil, and he will flee from you." Resist these enemy thoughts, do not meditate or act upon them, and they will not take root in your heart. Again, these are not your thoughts or intentions; they originate because the enemy wants to tempt you. Always remember that temptation is not a sign that you have done something wrong. Rather, it's an indication that you are on the right track and the enemy is intimidated by your progress. He aims to throw you off track.

Since we know that our thoughts will shape our actions, determine what we will submit to, what we will or will not do, and has the power to deceive us, how do we get a renewed mind? How do we frame new thought patterns? How do we detect the lies that the enemy has told us that we have believed? If we uncover the enemy's lies, then we can obtain the truth. Jesus tell us in John 8:31–32 that as we believe in Him, as we continue in His word, we will indeed become His disciples. As we become His disciples, the truth will be revealed, and it is this truth, *His truth*, that will make us free.

Renewing our minds frees us from everything that oppresses us. Whether it is fear, anxiety, rejection, unforgiveness, bitterness, or hurt, renewing our mind is what transforms the way we think and therefore changes who we are, how we behave, and how we interact. Renewing your mind is not just a process of exchanging your thoughts. It's not the process of simply thinking differently; it is so much more. In Romans 12:1–2, Paul says,

> I appeal to you therefore, brethren, and beg of you in view of [all] the mercies of God, to make a decisive dedication of your bodies [presenting all your members and faculties] as a living sacrifice, holy [devoted, consecrated] and well pleasing to God, which is your reasonable [rational, intelligent] service and spiritual worship. Do not be conformed to this world [this age], [fashioned after and adapted to its external, superficial customs], but be transformed [changed] by the [entire] renewal of your mind [by its new ideals and its new attitude], so that you may prove [for yourselves] what is the good and acceptable and perfect will of God, even the thing which is good and acceptable and perfect [in His sight for you]. (AMPC)

This lets us know that renewing our mind is a process of changing our ideals, customs, and attitude in order to conform to God's perfect and acceptable will and His views for us. In Ephesians 4:22–24, we are reminded not to simply change the way we think but to change our old behaviors, shed our old self, become new, and "put on our new self," which is the God-identity created in righteous and holy living. A renewed mind therefore has two requirements: (1) "to put off" any sin (any hurt, doubt, fear, rebellion, self-centeredness, lust, bitterness, etc.), any corrupt thinking, or any barrier that would offend God; and (2) putting on the mindset of Christ, which is the ideals in which God has designed for us to live by (2 Corinthians 10:5).[26]

Philippians 4:8–9 says,

> Finally, brethren, whatsoever things are true, whatsoever things are honest, whatsoever things are just, whatsoever things are pure, whatsoever things are lovely, whatsoever things are of good report; if there be any virtue, and if there be any praise, ***think on these things*** (emphasis mine). (KJV)

The context of the scripture reminds us to not be anxious or fearful; it instructs us on what we should be meditating on. So if you find yourself focusing on things that are impure, things that are hateful and ugly, things that lack moral integrity, things that promote pessimistic thinking, speak lies, or focus on bad reports and bad news, reexamine your thought life. As Philippians 4:7 says, God's peace will stand guard over all our thoughts and feelings (ERV).

Since I've learned that I am the sum of my thoughts, I find it essential to evaluate what I am meditating on any time I feel uneasy, worried, or not myself. During a time when I was relocating from one state to another, I found myself in deep worry and anxiety. Although I had relocated before, I was feeling a bit uneasy about whether I truly had the peace of God on the decision to move. My biggest concern was self-deception. I was so worried about doing things out of my own will that I felt my heart turn into a tailspin of unusual

---

[26] Nancy Missler, "What Is Mind Renewal & Why Is It So Important?: Be Ye Transformed," *Koinonia House* (February 1, 1996, retrieved July 15, 2020, from https://www.khouse.org/articles/1996/277/).

anxiety, worry, and panic. Even during my drive, I felt so much fear. I knew that it was not like me because I am usually bolder and fearless, but this time, I was bracing for disappointment and failure.

Normally, I would begin to pray. This time, however, I found it difficult to pray; I was already feeling like God was not going to answer me. The initial peace I had begun to wane. Although I received confirmation, I really wanted more "signs" from God. In this instance, I was struggling to clearly hear the mind of God because my fears were overpowering His voice.

When I finally got settled into my new place, God led me to John 14:18, which states that He would not leave me comfortless. I realized that I was experiencing a great deal of anxiety and discomfort because I allowed thoughts over past failures to overcloud my new season. I allowed the enemy to magnify my past experiences and write the narrative for my upcoming days. However, once I realized this and examined my thoughts, I realized how many lies I was believing. I realized how much I was not living in the promises of God and that the only deception that I was under was the enemy's fear.

This is why it's so important to know who you are in God. The enemy only comes to kill, steal, and destroy. The only way he could have stolen my peace is if I possessed peace to begin with. I began to meditate on the promises of God, and I was able to reclaim my peace and continue to prosper in my new location in my new season.

Remember, if your thoughts do not align with the Word of God, reexamine where they came from. Detect what is motivating your thoughts.

Stop and Reflect

It's time to flush out the bad and welcome the new. Get ready to do the hard work…

1. Identify areas of blockage that may exist in your life (unforgiveness, fear, procrastination, rejection, lack of transparency, insecurities, people-pleasing, etc.). How can you

release these areas to God? Write an example for each area you identify as a blockage.

2. Determine all negative thought patterns. Are all these thoughts your own? Are they God-thoughts (meaning driven by His Word) or thoughts from the enemy?

3. Examine if you are speaking in a way that glorifies God and edifies your renewed mind. Is what you are saying with your tongue indicating a renewed or an old way of thinking?

4. Identify if there are any areas in which you may be walking in deception because you have decided to follow your heart instead of the Word of God.

Now create and frame some new thoughts

Write a list of new thought patterns you can practice in order to renew your mind. This list can be exhaustive, so take your time and focus on what you should be thinking, how God wants you to think, and on every optimistic thing that is possible. For example, you can write out declarations such as "I am not in scarcity; I have more than enough. I have the mind of Christ. I am not a failure. I am beautiful. I have more than enough money because the Lord is my shepherd and I shall not lack. I have the talent, skill-set, and wisdom that I need," etc.

Remember, God wants you to live and think like Him. Anything that is not from Him is deception.

I Jumped!

I jumped!

I could not pinpoint how far I'd fall or if a net or chute would catch me.

All I knew is how danger felt, disappointment smelled, and how hard uncertainty clutched me.

Still, I inched closer to the rough edge of doubt, inhaled a gulp of faith, and shut my eyes tightly.

Like prey I felt hunted, paralyzed, but confronted by bewilderment eager to maul me.

Yet I was determined to overthrow the reign of impossibility, walk through clarity's door, and meet the King of Unpredictable.

To delight in ambiguity, permit fear to speak fluently, would dishonor my hope, be treason, be despicable.

But you must know, fear offered me a contract, to be my shield and defense in exchange to rule my comfort zone.

I signed over my rights to see, to dream…for cozy shackles, shiny fetters, and a new lover, who vowed to never leave me all alone.

Its power was ruthless, deceptive, and strong, but this time… I was determined to break free.

I dared to escape, ignore the whispers of hate that fear said was waiting and would always have its mark on me.

But there was only one way to be convinced, to be certain, downright factual, positive without doubt

That fear was a clever liar, a thief and a robber, a deceiver whose power needed to be taken out.

You see, I blindly walked the plank of hope before, chained by anxiety, muzzled by trepidation, bound by timidity, and held captive by my soul mate.

I watched as fear dangled defeat in front of me, cast failure on a rod to confuse me, spinning and reeling me in with embarrassment as bait.

So, one might ask, how could I launch out again into the blackness, into the deep, into the abyss of unfathomable space?

Because it is only there that the agenda of fear is nullified, made powerless, by perfect love and unfailing grace.

So could I stand the possibility of being disappointed again, take the plunge and descend into the gulf of the unknown?

Could I, the Queen of Control, let go and decapitate this ferocious monster, and his kingdom dethrone?

So I jumped...dry-mouthed, cracked throat, shaking hands, and chattering teeth.

I jumped...stomach failing, head throbbing, skin burning, and dangling feet.

I jumped...initially thinking that this taste of faith was just a little too salty,

Not knowing I would land into the hands of the one they call Strong and Mighty!

Fear, the impostor, was in for a surprise because it wasn't against me, this time, that he would be fighting.

When I leaped, I broke my treaty with fear and embraced the King of Kings who took over this freedom fight for me.

It's in His presence that I now rest, without fear's definitions and limitations hindering me.

I cast all of my cares on the One who shares my grief, comforts me, and knows me the most.

He's made me free and protected; we are one and connected, intertwined; "Fear Not," says the Lord of hosts.

So now I've kicked my old sweetheart to the curb and showed him what a date with faith looks like.

And at times when my old jealous lover flirts with me, I show him my new friend, because he doesn't want this fight!

Because I'll jump!

Chapter 8

Game Time

A Shot in the Dark

Have you ever walked into a familiar but dark room, reached for the light switch, and not find it in the exact place you predicted? Did you have to keep reaching and scaling the wall, hoping that you didn't trip and bump into something that would stub your toe, scratch, or poke you? It's not that you have never been in that room before, but navigating through the darkness throws off your sense of precision and awareness. Or have you ever played a game where you were blindfolded and had to hit a piñata or trust someone to catch you? What do all of these experiences have in common? Risk of the unknown and the prerequisite of having faith.

So far, we've discussed what can steal your identity, how your mistakes do not define you, how to prepare once you've been knocked down, how your heart can affect your perception of your identity, and what things can block or stagnate your progress. Once you have dealt with these issues, you must begin to transition into "your new self," which requires charting into new, uncomfortable territory and learning how to apply faith in every direction, especially within your identity.

So you have "shot your shot" and decided to trust God to transition you and recreate you into what He wants you to be. You've asked Him to come into your life, reveal your true identity and calling, and completely transform you. Your next question is, now what? The simple answer is "wait."

What is it like to wait on God? What is it like to want to hear His voice? How does it feel when you can't control what you can't predict? What does it mean to truly put your trust in God? Waiting on God means accepting uncertainty while maintaining complete trust. It means risking it all, even the possibility of failure, while conditioning your mind to expect that success is eminent. It seems paradoxical to trust God because you literally have to leave all plans up to Him while throwing out what you know has worked for you in the past. The past methods you used to get you where you currently are, are only good enough to help you maintain your current status. You must allow God to process you differently.

When God wants to transform you, He usually does things completely different than what you would expect. Your faith must take you to a place where you are challenged beyond your ordinary thought processes. You have to leap off of a cliff, knowing that God is your only safety net, even when there is no clear safety net in sight.

Timeout

One of the things that we must remember is that trusting in God has no time constraints. It's as if God is saying that He'll arrive at your situation at 7:00 p.m.; you believe Him, but the clock is stuck ticking repeatedly at 6:59 p.m. It's like He's decided to take a timeout while you are still in the game blindfolded.

I once was facing a difficult season, and knowing my identity in Christ, I asked God what I thought was a simple question: "Are Thou not God?" I literally asked Him if He was who He said He was. I could not understand that if God was *actually* God, how and why was I going through that situation for so long? However, God's response to me was twofold: "Are thou not My child?" and "I know who I am and who you are, but do you?" It was an immediate slap in the face. Here I was sitting and thinking that I understood my identity, and I knew who I was in Christ, when really, I was in doubt.

God simply revealed to me that not only did I not know who He really was, I also didn't know who I really was.

God began to show me how much He knew about me and how little I knew about myself. He began to reveal to me the details of everything that He was already working out for me, even as I was blinded by my own lack of faith and time constraints.

In John chapter 11, Lazarus was already dead by the time Jesus arrived. When Mary and Martha cried out about Jesus being too late in order to do anything about Lazarus's death, He responded to Mary and Martha by saying that *He **was** the resurrection*. He was not only able to come late but He was able to "step on" time, operate outside of its logical dimensions, and defeat it. In other words, Jesus intentionally allowed all time to expire, which gave God the glory when He raised Lazarus from the dead. By this action, there was no doubt of the power, mercy, and glory of God.

Sometimes, God will allow all your time to expire. He will allow the situation to extend far beyond your expectation of recovery just to show you who He really is. He knows better than us how to humble the proud, teach patience and endurance, and help us walk in faith and victory. In order to walk out our lives in our identity, we must not fear but with patience hope for what we cannot see (Romans 8:24–25).

God Is a Team Player

One of the greatest qualities about God is that He is both your coach and a team player. He gets dirty and gets into the fight with you all while encouraging you and guiding you to success.

God doesn't want us to struggle in our identity or in our faith in Him. He would rather us simply trust Him to reveal to us His plan. One thing that God promised us is that He will never leave us or forsake us. In Deuteronomy 31:8, Moses speaks to Joshua about God, saying, "And the Lord, he [It is] that doth go before thee; he will be with thee; he will not fail thee; neither forsake thee; fear not, neither be dismayed" (KJV).

The definition of *forsake* is "to abandon, desert, leave, reject, disown, or turn one's back on."[27] To fail means "to neglect to do something."[28]

> It is the Lord who goes before you; He will
> [march] with you; He will not fail you or let you
> go or forsake you; [let there be no cowardice or
> flinching, but] fear not, neither become broken
> [in spirit-depressed, dismayed, and unnerved
> with alarm]. (Deuteronomy 31:8 AMPC)

In this scripture, Moses was relaying God's instructions to Joshua from God prior to Joshua leading the children of Israel over to Jordan, which we also call the Promised Land. He was mentally preparing Joshua's mind, will, and emotions for what could have been a daunting task. Moses reminded Joshua that he wasn't alone because God had already gone before them; meaning, God had already guaranteed and ensured their success, prior to their arrival.

This is important to understand concerning your identity because any time you approach a new season, transition, or a new period in your life, or even while you are journeying through a current season, you must remember God is a team player and He has promised to never leave or forsake you. You must be mentally prepared and have your will and your emotions disciplined enough to understand that God has already ensured your success.

This does not mean that everything you do will be successful. Rather all things will work for your good in the end, according to Romans 8:28. He will not abandon you, desert you, leave you, reject you, disown you, or turn His back on you. His Word also says that He will not fail you; meaning, He will not neglect you in any area. What's more golden is that God does not want you to walk in cowardice or to flinch, which means "to make quick, nervous move-

---

27 *Oxford Dictionary*, s.v. "forsake" (retrieved January 7, 2019, from https://www.lexico.com/en/definition/forsake).

28 *Oxford Dictionary*, s.v. "fail" (retrieved January 7, 2019, from https://www.lexico.com/en/definition/fail).

ments, or to avoid doing something out of fear and anxiety."[29] He wants you to be sure of yourself because it is He, and His Spirit, that dwells within you. He gives us confidence and assurance as the fruit of righteousness, according to Isaiah 32:17.

Ultimately, He wants us to know that when He says that He won't leave us or forsake us, this applies to all things and every area of our life. We can literally insert whatever thing we are facing in the blank and declare that "God won't leave me, forsake me, or abandon me concerning _____, my identity, my household, my finances, my spiritual growth and maturity, my health…and He won't leave me without resources, without faith…" etc. Plainly, God is saying to us, "I got you!" He doesn't want us to worry but to trust His process for our complete identity transition.

On the Sidelines: Transition

One of the hardest periods in life is what I call the transition period. Transitions periods usually occur during a milestone, such as going through puberty, turning thirty, forty, or fifty; getting married, buying a home, or during your "coming of age" stages between seventeen and twenty-five. It is a period marked by change, expectation, and reflection.

Typically, this period can be the most difficult for a person who is struggling to know who they are. Without guidance, a person can make lifelong decisions that completely alter their view of the world. If not careful, a person can go into unusual pride, self-will, and marked stubbornness. They may have an unwillingness to submit themselves to the authority or wisdom of others. I also believe that people experience increased depression, suicidal ideation, increased vulnerability, midlife crises, and sometimes even homelessness during these periods. It's also common for "orphan spirits" to reemerge in an attempt to confuse and throw a person off course. Some may engage

---

[29] *Oxford Dictionary*, s.v. "flinch" (retrieved January 7, 2019, from https://www.lexico.com/en/definition/flinch).

in reckless behavior that masks their pain, sorrow, confusion, and lack of direction.

This is the period where a person may really need a lifeline but are blinded to the ones available. They may be required to follow the instructions of someone, but their own adult pride or immaturity won't allow them to submit. They are more focused on what brings them pleasure, comfort, and happiness than on what will benefit them in the long run.

Transition periods are the periods in life where you need to trust God the most. If not careful, you will find yourself not in the game of faith at all. You will be sitting on the sidelines watching life move on without you, while you grow tired, weary, and depressed. Any time you have reached a goal or are facing a transition, it is imperative that you refocus and seek God for your next steps. Don't let success convince you that "you've arrived" and don't let disappointments convince you that you aren't successful.

While you are patiently awaiting God for your next move, focus on who you are in Him and not on what hasn't yet occurred. Seek wise counsel. Counsel is defined as "advice, especially given formally, a policy or plan of action, deliberation, consultation, discussion for guidance, a lawyer."[30] God is the best counselor alive but there is also something to be said about seeking the wisdom of wise, trusted advisors in your life. As Proverbs 11:14 says, "Where there is no counsel, the people fall; But in the multitude of counselors there is safety" (NKJV).

Calculated Risks

A trained athlete knows how to calculate risks before they make any move in a game. They understand that each move they make is a risk that is either going to bring them closer to their goal or further away. A calculated risk is the act of exposing oneself to the possibility of opportunity, achievement, or success, after tallying the chances of

---

[30] *Oxford Dictionary*, s.v. "counsel" (retrieved July 6, 2020, from https://www.lexico.com/en/definition/counsel).

defeat, peril, or failure. It's not simply weighing the pros and cons of a situation but the process of using logical reasoning to make informed choices with anticipated results.

When you are transitioning into "the new," it's common to depend upon old logic, old ways of reasoning, and old decision-making processes to reach conclusions. However, when God does a new thing, its's typically outside of your comfort zone. Sometimes, He will challenge you to come out of your personality and preferences in order to come into your new identity in Him. Although this transition is a calculated risk in some sorts, it really requires you to move into "new wine skins" or what I call "the new."

How many times have you heard a person say that they refuse to do something because it's not within their personality or it's not what they would normally do? It is human nature to simply live life as you always have, with your preferences and personality type as the driving force. However, changing requires you to move beyond what you may prefer, what may seem comfortable, cozy, and even easy. Luke 5:37–38 draws a picture of a parable that explains that no one puts new wine into old wineskins because it will burst the skins, spill the wine, and both the skins and wine will be destroyed. New wine must be put into new wineskins so that the wine and the skins are both preserved.

Isaiah 43:18–19 is also a great reference to consider when God is transitioning you into something new. It says to "not remember the former things or the things of old because God will do a new thing." He will even do things that seem impossible such as make a way in the wilderness and create rivers in the desert. When God is setting you up on a new path of transition, He wants you to understand that He's already made all of the necessary calculations. Your job is to trust Him to go into the new, leaving the limitations of your comfort zone behind while not allowing your old safety nets to enslave you.

Keep Your Head in the Game

The danger of relying consistently on our own logic is that we don't know all that we think we know. When we begin reasoning, we start with stating, "I already know that ____will happen," or "This can't work because____," or "All I've ever seen or experienced is___." This defeated or limiting attitude blinds us to all of the possibilities of God and the exceptions that He makes for those in whom He favors.

Sometimes when we lack clarity, it is because we have asked God to do "exceedingly above all that we can ask or think." Because He loves us, He wants to do this for us, and therefore we cannot perceive His next move. When we are in the dark about some of His plans, it only gives Him more glory once we trust Him completely.

Keeping your head in the game is about expanding your thinking and your faith on what you think is possible. If there is something that you have been seeking God about and it is based off what you know or have seen, you may be missing the unprecedented blessing that God has waiting for you. God doesn't want us to think "small" but would rather us activate faith in every area of our lives. He is still a miracle-working God.

Let us remember to not mistake a lack of clarity for spiritual blindness. Sometimes things are concealed to shield you and your enemy from what God is doing. Although God takes pleasure in revealing things (according to Deuteronomy 29:29 and Amos 3:7), sometimes He withholds details for your protection. Do not mistake what I am saying; God reveals secrets and informs His prophets of things to come. However, He doesn't always share every element with us when we desire to know more. Continue to seek Him. A lack of clarity is not synonymous with blindness because God can see in the dark. He requires us to be patient, to trust Him, and to endure in seasons when we cannot clearly see what's next in our lives. Remain focused and keep your head in the game.

Bonus Shot, Free Throw, or Foul?

Knowing your identity is so important in your walk of faith because not knowing leaves you vulnerable to pessimism and the dreaded "orphan mentality." It also leaves you wondering if God really cares about you. Not being rooted in your identity sets you up to miss what I like to call "bonus shots" or the favor of God. When I was facing some difficult situations, I began to question, "Can I ask God for a favor that is not a need? Does God's grace run out when my faith runs out?" In other words, there were things that I desired that I didn't feel were necessarily a "big deal" to God. So I questioned whether it was worth it for me to have faith for things that I viewed as small.

For example, I had an upcoming event where I was asked to host. Although I had quite a few things in my closet, I didn't feel that I had anything appropriate to wear, or at least that I wanted to wear. Does God really care that I want something new? It's not exactly a need, and surely God has bigger things to worry about, right? Like curing cancer, healing someone's lungs, sparing a baby, or feeding the impoverished? Another example is that I wanted my kids to attend a certain private school because I thought that it would benefit them in the future. However, they certainly could attend public school free, so does God really care that I didn't have the money at the time for the private school? Why would God answer my prayers for something so selfish or frivolous when He can focus on something bigger like sparing the life of a sick person?

So it begs the question, are these things worth having faith for? We already know that He's not some type of Santa Claus who exists to fulfil our desires at whim. So does God dole out blessings based on worthiness or on how big or small the problem is? The short answer is "No!" So, does God's grace run out when I lack faith for seemingly small issues? No! God answers us according to His plan and His will, not according to our logic on whether or not He should answer us at all.

When you don't know who you are, you rely on logic to determine your worthiness. God is a good father and favors us and gives us good gifts just because He can and because He wants to, according to Matthew 7:11. When you know your identity in Him, you will come to understand that it's not the thing that you want that makes something a "big deal;" God sees you as a "big deal" simply because you are His son or daughter. He answers the righteous cries of *His* people and He takes pleasure in making the **bonus shots for us!**

However, if what we desire is not according to His will, no matter how big, small, or frivolous, we just can't have it. If this happens, how should we respond? Does this mean that God doesn't love us? Of course not! We know that God still loves us. But how do you cope when your feelings still feel like He doesn't? What happens when in your heart you feel unloved because despite knowing, and acknowledging the truth, that God does actually love you, you still feel as if He doesn't? This is a clear indication of an identity issue and a lack of renewing your mind. When you know your identity, you will have emotional stability and you will know, acknowledge, and live in **the truth** about something even when you *feel* the opposite. It's making the decision to not allow your feelings to rule you or your heart. It is the process of bringing your feelings into alignment with the truth that rests on the inside.

Contrarily, what happens when you have a desire for something that **is** an *actual* need, but your motives for wanting it are impure? God would declare, "Foul!" For example, you may need money for your life, family, education, kids, etc. These are real, legitimate needs. Let's say that in this example, you don't desire a prosperous career to fulfill these needs but instead you really want a prosperous career so that you can have self-security in the money you earn and validation of your worth and skills. If your identity is rooted in Christ, then your security and validation should also be rooted in Him and not in your own personal performance or ambition. However, because we live in a performance-driven society, it often proves difficult for us to separate who we are from what we do.

So does this mean that God will not give me what I need until I solve the issues connected to my motives? A lot of times, this is exactly what happens. What's interesting about this conundrum is that you must realize that your needs do not outweigh your purpose. Often, because we feel that our needs are imminent, we will set aside pursing our identity and our purpose to fulfil our needs. However, God will prioritize your personal deliverance over your needs because your deliverance is connected to your destiny. He is committed to your wholeness more than anything that you need. Although His promise to take care needs is not nullified by our actions, your answers to your needs can be delayed by your unwillingness to deal with motives of your desires.

In my life, when I didn't know my identity, when I hadn't been introduced to the "new me" yet, and when it was taking longer than I anticipated to learn my identity, I ambitiously pursued my career because I knew that it would meet my immediate needs. I figured that I could worry about my purpose later. However, I ran into a major problem because none of the career choices I made were actually fulfilling. In fact, I intentionally made fulfilling my needs my purpose.

For you, it may not be a career, but a family, a business, a marriage, a relationship, money, or something else. The issue with thinking that I could put off my purpose to pursue something else, was that what if the career that God wanted me to have, I wasn't yet qualified for, because I didn't know myself?

What if I only looked at job descriptions based on what I thought I could do, based on my current skill set and ability, without realizing that I didn't yet know all of my skill sets and abilities? What if I was struggling with operating in my identity because I was using the pursuit of my career to deflect from my real issues so that I wouldn't have to learn who I was meant to be? What if knowing my identity would lead me to developing the new skill sets and abilities that I needed to perform well in my new career? God wants us to operate from identity, in our identity, and not work for it. We do not have to work to be a son or daughter. We are simply justified by faith.

God will move on your purpose (the whole reason He put you on the earth) before He will meet your needs in your timing. I had to realize that if I sought to know my identity, my needs would be met as a byproduct of that pursuit. However, you might ask, what if it takes a long time to mature or be ready for purpose or the pursuit thereof; do your needs then get completely neglected? No. Because we do not always know the will of heaven, we should ask for both what we need and what we want, taking the free throw and the bonus shot; because although we are not guaranteed to have both all of the time, we are definitely guaranteed to not have what we don't ask for.

When I lacked confirmation in who I was in Christ, I made the habit of pursing my career based on my needs and qualifications. This spilled over into other areas of my life as well. However, making a pursuit based on my needs never actually resulted in me getting all that I wanted or needed. I was always left with a limited amount of fulfillment and never ultimately got the results I was looking for in the long-term. In fact, as soon as I started a new career, I would have money, take care of my bills and immediate needs, and soon find myself bored and unfulfilled. I would be ready for a new job and be facing another cycle of the same thing. I had to change my perception and understand that if I focused on purpose, God would focus on my needs because my purpose is His righteousness, His kingdom, and *for* His glory.

I realized that I was going through repeated cycles because I had been continuously pursuing my needs and not digging deep enough to get to know Him. The more you know God, the more you know yourself, because as born-again believers, we are made in His image. Although we are all God's creation, we are not all God's children. His children are made in His image.[31] I will discuss this more in detail in chapter 10. If we do not pursue relationship with God, He can't reveal our purpose. Not that He's unable to but He won't permit Himself to, as an act of His own will. He would rather protect us from ourselves, our poor motives, and our bad decisions.

If we develop all of our talents, skills, and abilities, on our own, we can be convinced out of our purpose because we will believe we are qualified for it, based on something we've done. We will think that our success was based on our own efforts and logic alone. However, if God divinely imparts to us His wisdom, gifts, and skills, and allows us to develop more because of His will, His grace, and His purpose, we will not doubt that we acquired these things by God. Therefore, we cannot be convinced out of the purpose God has given us because we didn't get "there" by ourselves.

---

[31] R. Watson Jr., "Foundations Class, Part 4: Faith" (July 1, 2019).

Hit or Miss: Are Your Prayers Being Heard?

What is the point of praying if you do not get answers? How many times have you sought the Lord about something and felt ignored? Is it possible to confidently pray and expect God to answer you? To answer these questions, we first must deal with what prayer actually is.

Many Christians approach prayer in a way that rarely gets them the answers they are seeking. They have a hit-and-miss relationship with how often God answers them. This is because many believe that prayer is simply pouring out one's heart to God. Well, I have got bad news for you. If you have simply poured out *your heart* to God, then you have not actually prayed. The main purpose of prayer is to get answers, which means prayer can be done incorrectly. We know that this is a fact because in Luke 11:1–3, one of Jesus's disciples asked Him to teach them to pray.

> And it came to pass, that, as he was praying in a certain place, when he ceased, one of his disciples said unto him, Lord, teach us to pray, as John also taught his disciples. And he said unto them, When ye pray, say, Our Father which art in heaven, Hallowed be thy name. Thy kingdom come. Thy will be done, as in heaven, so in earth. (KJV)

In Matthew 6:5–15, we see a similar parallel. If prayer was simply pouring out one's heart and feelings to God, the disciples would not have asked Jesus to teach them how to do it. It's amazing that the disciples witnessed Jesus perform miracles, and even performed them themselves, but the one thing they asked to be taught was how to pray.

Simply put, prayer is the technology that heaven uses to transport heaven to earth. Therefore, the goal of our prayers should be to bring the existence of heaven to the existence of our lives here on earth. Note that the scripture says, "Thy kingdom come" and "Thy will be done on earth as it is in heaven" (Matthew 6:10).

In order to pray effectively, we must debunk some common myths. Some of the myths surrounding prayer is that God doesn't answer prayers, God says no to prayers, and God says "wait" to prayers. Another myth is that all prayers are the same. This is untrue because there are "prayers of faith," which only require you to pray for something once; there are prayers of intercession, where you implement the "knock, seek, and ask" principles, which means you go back multiple times for the same thing; there are prayers of supplication, where you are entreating God and appealing to Him for certain petitions; there are prayers of thanksgiving; and a time for repentance. This list is not exhaustive but depending on the type of prayer you are engaging in, the rules can change.

Since the Word of God is the final authority on how Christians live, we must examine what it says about God and our relationship with prayer. First John 5:14–15 says,

> And this is the confidence that we have in him, that, if we ask **any thing according to his will**, _he heareth us_: And if we know that he hears us, whatsoever we ask, we know that we have the petitions that we desired of him. (KJV, emphasis mine)

This scripture tells us that if we pray boldly according to God's will, He will "hear" us. This means we can conclude that any prayer that we pray that is not according to God's will, He cannot hear. It's not that He cannot hear because He's unable to, rather He chooses not to Hear because the prayer is not according to His divine will. How can God answer a prayer that He has never "heard"? The scriptures goes on to point out, that _if_ he **hears us**, we **will** have the petitions that we have asked of Him.

It is crucial that we understand that this scripture is an "if/then" statement. Anytime we see the word _if_, we know what we will receive is based on the contingency of what we do. If your prayers are not being answered, it likely means that you are not praying according to God's will. These prayers, according to James 4:2–3, are described as amiss.

> Yet you don't have what you want because you don't ask God for it. And even when you ask, you don't get it because your motives are all wrong—you want only what will give you pleasure [or what fulfils your own desires]. (NLT)

This means that the only thing I have to do to get my prayers answered is to get God to hear them to begin with. What this tells us is that the ONLY answer to prayers is yes. God doesn't say no to our prayers that are in alignment with His will, but He will say no to the desires of our heart if our motives are impure. John 14:13–14 says, "And whatsoever ye shall ask in my name, that will I do, that the Father may be glorified in the Son. If ye shall ask any thing in my name, I will do it" (KJV). This lets us know that **anything** that we ask in the Lord's name that is according to **His will**, He will answer with yes.

Every time we pray, we should be praying confidently and boldly because we understand that as long as we are praying according to God's will, we will get the answers that we seek. This is such a relief because knowing how to pray properly can prevent us from having a hit-and-miss relationship with prayer. So your next question might be, how do I find the will of God? Romans 12:1–2 lets us know that the will of God must be discerned through a renewed mind. As we mentioned before, James 1:21 lets us know it is only the Word of God that is "engrafted" or "implanted" in us that can save our souls.

Do not forget that the definition of the soul is the mind, will, and emotions. Therefore, any thought that we have that does not have a root-system in the Word of God, needs to be renewed. Determining the will of God involves researching and learning His Word. God's voice sounds just like His Word. If you do not know His Word, you definitely cannot discern His will. Discerning His will help you differentiate between your plans and His.

Ask yourself, how do you know when your plan is not in sync with God's? What are the results of your plans? How have they helped or hurt you? You can literally research every scripture that speaks of God's will to learn more about Him. However, this is only a starting point. Only dedicated devotion to God and time spent in His Word will help you hear His voice and determine His will more clearly.

However, as I mentioned before, there are different rules to prayer. Let's say one wanted to pray to "move a mountain" in one's life, according to Mark 11:22–24, which states,

> And Jesus answering saith unto them, Have faith in God. For verily I say unto you, That whosoever shall say unto this mountain, Be thou removed, and be thou cast into the sea; and ***shall not doubt in his heart*** [emphasis mine], but shall believe that those things which he saith shall come to pass; he shall have whatsoever he saith. Therefore I say unto you, What things so ever ye desire, when ye pray, believe that ye receive them, and ye shall have them.

This scripture informs us that if you lack faith and have doubt in your heart, the mountain will not be moved. It's another statement based on the contingency of our behaviors. Also, you must understand that not only can you not have doubt, you must still pray according to His will before His answer will be yes! Another example is the prayer of faith found in James 5:15, which says, "And the prayer of faith shall save the sick, and the Lord shall raise him up; and if he have committed sins, they shall be forgiven him." This means that if you are desiring to heal someone and do not pray the "prayer of faith," or prayer found in faith, a person may remain in their sickness.

Lastly, in James 1:5–8, we find instructions on how to pray for wisdom.

> If any of you lack wisdom, let him ask of God, that giveth to all men liberally, and

upbraideth not; and it shall be given him. But let him ask in faith, nothing wavering. For he that wavereth is like a wave of the sea driven with the wind and tossed. For **let not that man think that he shall receive any thing of the Lord**. A double minded man is unstable in all his ways. (KJV, emphasis mine)

Notice how the scripture states that if we do not ask for wisdom in faith, if we waver in our confidence in asking Him, we are one who is "doubleminded" or one who lacks confidence that God is who He says He is. This scripture strictly points out that we will get "nothing" from God if this is our heart posture.

You may be thinking, what does how I pray have to do with my identity? Since we know according to John 16:23–27 that we are to pray to the Father in the name of Jesus, we must accept that we are sons communicating to our heavenly Father. If you have a wrong view of God and a distorted view of yourself, your prayer life will be unsuccessful. Your perspective impacts how you will approach God. For example, if you see yourself as a slave and God as your master, your prayer life will be unsuccessful. This is because we only have access to God since we are sons. He instructed us as sons to boldly approach the "the throne of Grace" (Hebrews 4:16). If we are coming to Him as slaves, then we are not operating in our identity.

When we are approaching God in prayer, we should not pray focused on our own righteousness but on God's. Remember, He gave us righteousness as a gift in exchange for our sins (2 Corinthians 5:21 and Romans 5:17). This means that starting off prayer with repentance is us praying according to our own righteousness. Although there are times when we need to repent, starting off every prayer with repentance forces us to focus on our own righteousness instead of understanding that when God sees us, since we pray to Him in the name of Jesus, He only sees His Son because His son took our place on the cross. Jesus didn't mention the forgiveness of "our debts and sins" until the prayer concluded.

Remember, as much as we believe that Jesus became our sins, God made us righteous. We should focus on praying to the Father on the credibility of Jesus's name and based on what Jesus has already done for us through justification. So should we repent? Yes, but repentance is not necessarily prayer. Repentance is when the Holy Spirit is trying to convict us of something and demonstrate to us that there is a part of our lives that we are still trying to live based on our own merit. Jesus came not to condemn the world (John 3:17), so feelings of condemnation only brings us to a place of guilt. This guilt pushes us away from God, whereas conviction brings us back into the grace of God and makes us aware of our potential and identity in Him.

Therefore, we should search the scriptures on how to pray about specific things to ensure that we are praying according to God's will. This will also help to ensure that we are approaching God, our Father, from the right perspective and within our authentic identity. This will help us achieve the results in prayer that we desire.

Defense

In order to deliberately win any game, a player needs to be aware of their defense strategy. Defense is defined as "the action of defending from or resisting attack; a means of protecting something from attack; and the action or role of defending one's goal against the opposition."[32] Having a successful defense strategy means being aware of one's blind spots and fears, and examining all default behavior.

Blinds spots are those areas in your life that are weaknesses that are not easily visible. These are the areas in which "a person's view is obstructed."[33] These areas are the most weak, sensitive zones, that are prone to become visible, only when "life happens," and when pressured is applied. Blind spots can be emotional, social, and psychological. They can take the form of "annoying habits like interrupting

[32] *Oxford Dictionary*, s.v. "defense" (retrieved July 20, 2020, from https://www.lexico.com/en/definition/defense).

[33] *Oxford Dictionary*, s.v. "blind spot" (retrieved July 20, 2020, from https://www.lexico.com/definition/blind_spot).

or bragging, [excessive talkativeness], [personality disorders] or, they might be deeper fears or desires that are too threatening to acknowledge."[34] These blinds spots are emphasized in your relationships with others and hide in personality weaknesses that you refuse to deal with.

Ultimately, they obstruct your ability to connect with God more deeply. This is because your identity development remains in an infant state, blocking you from seeing the areas in which you need to grow and develop. Blind spots also prevent you from seeing yourself in the way that God intends. God does not want any us blind in any area. He has designed for all of His children to access deliverance. Remember, as it says in Joel 2:32, "whosoever shall call on the name of the LORD shall be delivered." *Shall* means *shall*—not *maybe*, not *might*, and not *may*, but *shall*. If there are any areas in which you need deliverance, God is able to unshackle you from bondage.

When you are blind in any area, you will be unable to adequately defend and prepare yourself against the enemy's attacks. Every defense strategy and counteroffensive operation that the enemy uses is designed to take advantage of your weaknesses to gain an edge over you. He desires to extort your blind spots, making your strategies against him less effective. It's not that Satan is not already a defeated foe, because we know that he is, but your blind spots will block your ability to actively operate from an area of victory when your spiritual view is obstructed.

This is because your blind spots uncover how much you have partnered with the Holy Spirit and the Word of God to renew your mind. It is also because you cannot see the "new you" as long as your blind spots remain hidden. As the parable in Mark chapter 4 illuminates, if Word of God has not been rooted and planted in your heart, "the cares of [life and] this world" will reduce the Word of God in your life until it has no meaningful effect. If the Word of God doesn't rest within you, you will be carried away by the winds and storms that life brings your way. You will be unable to operate in greater faith because your blind spots often conceal hidden fears

---

[34] Juliana Breines, "Psychological blind spots," *Psych Your Mind* (August 19, 2011, retrieved July 20, 2020, from http://psych-your-mind.blogspot.com/2011/08/friday-fun-psychological-blind-spots.html).

and provide comfort for default behaviors. Since faith and fear are in polar opposite of each other, default behaviors hamper the development of your identity in Christ, which depends upon operating in great realms of faith.

One type of blind spot can be uncovered by our default, reflexive behaviors. Our default behaviors are our automatic responses to situations that seem natural to us. As we become new creatures in Christ, it is essential that we examine our default behavior. We must ask ourselves, "How do I respond when I get offended? How do I respond when I don't get my way? How do I respond when I'm unclear about what season I am living in? How do I respond when I'm angry, upset, confused, or don't understand something? How do I respond when I can't hear God? How do I respond when I feel left alone and forsaken?" As we process the answers to these questions, we have to come into total agreement and submission to everything that God is doing with us. This often requires us to give up our preference to have full knowledge of everything that God wants for us, prior to us committing to His processes.

We have to perfect our responses to Him and allow the Word of God to shape our identity. Perfecting our responses requires us to not only examine our default behavior but to mature spiritually and change the way we think and operate. We must learn to ignore the lies that the enemy tries to bring to us, understanding that as we renew our minds, the enemy desires to come and challenge our new belief systems. He hates for us to see and accept ourselves as sons and daughters of God, as heirs of God and joint heirs of Christ, in our rightful identity. He would rather us view ourselves as helpless mortals with little to no authority.

Another blind spot can be uncovered by examining what we fear the most. Although I have talked about fear several times, understanding what you fear the most reveals hidden emotions, wounds, and issues that are in direct conflict with your complete identity formation. Most of our fears come from past experiences or tainted wisdom given to us by others. We have to understand that our experiences do not have to give us direction or determine our future; they simply give us context for our past. Once we process what we fear the most, and examine our past experiences, we can then allow God to process us in the way that He uniquely designed for us to go through in this journey. Our process will never look like anyone else's process and our differences are what make us "us."

For example, one of the things that I feared the most was becoming the thing that I criticized. I feared remaining small and not advancing. I was observing others whom I thought truly wanted "greater" but never achieved anything but mediocrity. I was living stuck in comparison and false humility. I often thought…what makes me so special? Why do I believe that I can and will achieve everything that God has intended for me? How do I overcome the pride concerning what I am able to do versus what God wants to do through me? How do I overcome the rejection and fear of not being accepted or loved by others whom I valued? Where did I place the doubt of asking myself, *why me?* How do I walk completely free in the uniqueness that God created in me without feeling like I have to constantly explain myself to others? How do I find reassurance when I've never seen someone like me forge a path similar to mine?

All of these things break down to a fear of success. However, these things were all concealed under my blind spots. I often hesitated to commit to new things because of this fear. I wanted to stay comfortable in my fears, in my personality type, and in my comfort zone. This prevented me from truly launching out to discover everything that God intended for me to be. These fears also created a void that I tried to fill with temporary achievements. However, those voids always came back to whisper to my inner self. In order to become completely free and whole, I had to leap into what God wanted me to become and leave every fear, blind spot, and default behavior behind. Instead of focusing on what I was giving up, I finally could focus on everything God had for me to gain because my identity depended upon me releasing myself fully into God's plans.

Master Your Opponent

Knowing who you are playing against is a great strategy for winning your game. If you focus on each opponent as an individual entity, you can develop strategies that are tailored to win against a particular team. This will help ensure that you have the most successful season.

The biggest opponent you will face in your identity creation is different types of fear. I know that I have discussed fear so many times, but it is important to understand just how strongly the spirit of fear works against you and your identity. Remember that fear is the main vehicle that the enemy uses to keep you in the past, and faith is the main vehicle that God uses to get you to your future.

Fear has the ability to mask itself in such deceptive ways, it's a difficult opponent to master. It is always disguising itself and presenting itself creatively in different situations. The enemy can't use the future against you because he is not omniscient and he doesn't know your future. He uses trial and error and takes clues from how you respond in situations to try to figure out what's next for you. He then strategizes to keep you from realizing your victory. Every time we are faced with any type of fear, we must ask ourselves, what is the agenda of fear in this situation? Be certain that fear *always* has an agenda.

Fear is "a feeling, an unpleasant strong emotion, induced by perceived danger, or by the anticipation or awareness of a threat."[35] It is a spirit of deception that wants you to believe that you are in danger or that a threat is imminent. The purpose of fear is to paralyze you, keep you from moving, and exhaust you physically, mentally, and emotionally. It works tirelessly to keep you in bondage. If you are in fear, you cannot have a sound mind or make sound decisions. You will struggle to hear the mind of Christ because your fearful thoughts will overpower His. If you meditate on your fears, you cannot meditate or focus on the Word of God. Remember, if Jesus could sleep through the storm, we can do the same.

Fear is bondage, the state of being a slave. Since we have cried, "Abba, Father," meaning we have accepted Christ in our lives and are now living in Him, we have received His heavenly adoption into His family. We longer have to be a slave to fear. The entire assignment and agenda of fear is to rob us of power, love, and sound mental

---

[35] *Oxford Dictionary*, s.v. "fear" (retrieved August 20, 2020, from https://www.lexico.com/en/definition/fear).

health and stability (2 Timothy 1:7). Fear is not your friend; it is not simply anxiety or worry; it is literally a spirit from hell. Although it manifests in many different forms, it is still the same spirit.

If there is a manifestation of any type of fear in your life, whether it be worry, anxiety, panic, despair, insecurity, restlessness, or insomnia, it means that you have not sought God for deliverance as intensely as you need to in that area. Psalms 34:4 says, "I sought the Lord, and he heard me, and delivered me from all my fears." This is a great reminder that if you are intent on seeking the Lord, He will hear you, and He *will* deliver you from **ALL** of your fears. I understand that in today's society, it is common for people to treat their anxiety and panic attacks with medication. I am not advocating for anyone to ignore their doctor's advice, but I am encouraging every Christian to seek God for complete and total deliverance from every type of fear. Medication only abates fears temporarily, but it doesn't cure them. Supernatural deliverance through faith can completely destroy all works of fear.

First John 4:18 says, "There is no fear in love; but perfect love casts out fear, because fear involves torment. But he who fears has not been made perfect in love. We love Him because He first loved us" (KJV). This explains that when we are in fear, we will not love as we should. We become "fearful lovers" and cannot even love God the way that we should. God's perfect loves is what eliminates fear. Therefore, in order to completely eradicate fear, we must first receive God's perfect love in our heart. Do not forget, the ultimate goal of fear is to drive you further away from God and your identity and rob you of your purpose and your destiny. Fear is from Satan and therefore is enmity against God, "the state or feeling or being actively opposed or hostile to him [or his word.]"[36]

---

[36] Lexco.com (n.d.) Enmity: Definition of Enmity by Oxford Dictionary on Lexico.com also meaning of Enmity. Retrieved July 29, 2020 from https://www.lexico.com/en/definition/enmity.

Offense

Just as any good player understands the defense strategy in the game, no player can win without a brilliant offensive strategy. Offense is defined as "any legal action used to attack, advance or score."[37] Having an excellent offensive strategy requires being decided on who God is and who you are in Him. This means that you are trusting in Him with all of your heart, intensifying your focus, and not only having faith in Him but having the confidence that He is the "I Am" and He is "for you."

The first step to understanding who God is, is understanding that He is NOT something that you have created in your head. You cannot create a relationship with God that is built on your own limitations and understanding of Him. He is not like us. He operates beyond our thoughts, understanding, and even our knowledge of Him. Once you understand His sovereignty, you can learn to trust in Him with all of your heart, not base your thoughts and decisions on your own logic, and acknowledge Him by following His Word and His will, and only then will He guide you in all of your decisions (Proverbs 3:5–6).

Technically, Ephesians 6:10 does not tell us to fight but tells us to "be strong in the Lord, and in the power of his might." If you do not understand who is fighting your battles for you, you will rest upon your own ability to succeed. It's much easier to trust in God who is "for you," as it says in Romans 8:31, than it is to trust in a god made with hands. The scripture also asks us that if God is for us, who can be (or win) against us? In context, this scripture is not saying that nothing bad can happen to you or that you won't lose at certain things in life; it is saying that our relationship with God is secured in Christ's redemptive power of love and grace. It's saying that no matter what bad things come our way, God still loves us deeply and nothing can separate us from the love that He has for us.

---

[37] Lexico.com (n.d.) Offense: definition of Offense by Oxford Dictionary on Lexico.com also meaning of Offense. Retrieved July 20, 2020, from https://www.lexico.com/en/definition/offense.

Trusting in the Lord with all of your heart prompts you to ask yourself if there is anything too hard for God (Jeremiah 32:27, Genesis 18:14). Once you understand that God can defeat all and every impossibility, it's easier to completely trust and depend on His abilities and not your own. There is a significant difference between having faith in God and having confidence that He will do it for you, whatever your "it" may be.

I have often heard people talk about how much faith they have in God. They feel as if their faith in God is very strong and they often claim, "He is able." Having total faith in God is not just trusting in His ability to do something. It's not just claiming that "He is able." It is having the confidence that not only is He able but He's going to do it for me. When someone trusts in God's ability but does not believe that He *is* going to do something for them, it is because they have a subtle type of unbelief. This sort of unbelief was painted in an allegorical picture described in Matthew 17:14–21.

The story is about a man who came to Jesus for the healing of his son. He had initially brought his son to Jesus's disciples, but they were unable to heal him. Jesus healed the man's son and cast out the spirit that made him ill. Afterward, Jesus's disciples came to Him in private and asked Him why they could not cast the spirit out of the child and heal him. Jesus responded that it was because of their unbelief.

Now at first glance on reading this scripture, it may be easy to assume that the disciples didn't have any faith at all. Well, the fact that they healed the sick and cast out spirits before this situation occurred proves to us that it wasn't the fact that they didn't have *any* faith. Rather, it was the fact that they didn't have the type of faith needed to cast out this spirit. This is the type of faith that keeps on growing. Notice how in verses twenty and twenty-one, Jesus says, "If ye have faith as a grain of mustard seed, ye shall say unto this mountain, Remove hence to yonder place; and it shall remove; and nothing shall be impossible unto you. Howbeit this kind goeth not out but by prayer and fasting" (KJV).

Jesus instructed them that they needed to have faith "as a grain of mustard seed." Often, we as Christians focus on the size of the mustard seed, believing that it is okay to have small faith as long as it is the "size of a mustard seed." However, Jesus often rebuked people for having small faith. He would say things such as "O ye of little faith." Jesus wasn't giving them permission to have little faith but to have faith "as a grain of mustard seed." What does it mean to have faith as a grain of mustard seed? In Matthew 13:31–32, the scripture tells us,

> Another parable put he forth unto them, saying, The kingdom of heaven is like to a grain of mustard seed, which a man took, and sowed in his field: Which indeed is the least of all seeds: but when it is grown, it is the greatest among herbs, and becometh a tree, so that the birds of the air come and lodge in the branches thereof.

If the kingdom of heaven is like a grain of mustard seed, this lets us know that Jesus was talking about having faith that grows. Even if our faith starts off small, when it is planted and takes root, no matter how small, it should be growing into a tree in which others can feed. This tells us that our faith should be growing so much and so strong that even others should be able to benefit from the faith that we have.

This also lets us know that there is a type of unbelief that can creep in and keep your faith from growing. We often build monuments around what God has already done, and this transforms into unbelief. We say things such as "God did this for me before, so I know He can do this for me again." However, comparing what God has done to what He can do can be a grave mistake because God can perform exceedingly and abundantly above all that you can ask or think. Although He wants us to be grateful, He doesn't want us to create a monument around the things that He has done and only worship Him with a mindset based off the past.

God wants us to have faith that grows so we can believe in Him for things that are yet to come. When we focus only on what He has done to create a reference for what He can do, we limit God and allow subtle unbelief to creep in. In fact, Jesus said that this type of subtle unbelief is only overcome through a combination of fasting and prayer. This is because fasting protects your anticipation of what God will do and not just what He has already done. When we have faith "as a grain of a mustard seed," and not as the *size* of a grain of mustard seed, Jesus says that "nothing will be impossible to us." This type of faith gives us the freedom to leave our comfort zones. As an act of our will, we will permit the Holy Spirit to come in and take our training wheels off, so that we can learn how to balance in faith without the crutch of using the old things that God has already done to lean on. We can grow and expand into dimensions that we never thought possible.

Faith is not automatically in us but comes to us through the Word of God (Romans 10:17). Since faith comes by hearing the word (*rhema*) of God, we understand that we cannot have faith that doesn't come into our hearts. Once faith comes to us, we must make a decision to allow faith to come in, and then we have to become decided on what Jesus has said to us, whether through His word or through *rhema*. Being decided about what Jesus said allows us to then release faith through our mouth. We will begin to use the power of our tongue to speak life to the things God said and believe Him so that those things manifests in our lives. Faith is not about denying reality but about choosing as an act of your will to change the way you think and speak until you see change manifest. Faith is simply taking God at His Word. Our entire identity rests on faith because faith is what gives us access to the Father and it is in Him where everything we need resides.

Once we have recognized our blind spots, defeated the agenda of fear, and learned how to have faith that grows, we can then intensify our focus on moving forward. Intensifying our focus means becoming more cognizant of distractions; it means learning how to be more disciplined and committed to surrendering to God's plan and His identity for us. It means becoming decided about our process and allowing God's transformation process to have free course in our lives. The more focused and disciplined we become, the more we will be able to connect and hear from God. His plans for our lives will be more evident, and the clarity that we have always longed for will manifest in miraculous ways.

Stop and Reflect

Jump into God and out of your limitations...

1. Have you put your complete trust in God for every situation in your life? If so, how can you be sure? If not, why? What can you do to completely lean on God and trust Him more?
2. In what areas have you not jumped or taken a leap of faith (i.e., in your business, relationships, savings, education, weight loss, goals, etc.)? Are you still sitting on the sidelines? If so, why?
3. Identify areas in which you went into a place of doubt because something didn't happen within the timeframe that you expected. In what ways can you continue to have faith for a victory not yet realized?
4. How have your personal preferences limited you from stepping outside of your comfort zone?
5. Examine whether you have been praying according to God's will. Are you getting consistent yeses to your prayers? If not, how can you reconstruct your prayer life?
6. Examine your default behavior and blind spots. Do you run when you can't get your way? Do you retreat, fight, argue, or give up when things do not go as planned? Do you sell yourself short when you feel lonely, unloved, or abandoned? Do you pick up negative thought patterns when you are rejected?
7. In what ways can you master your opponent?

Chapter 9

Can You Hear Him?

God Speaks

Hearing the voice of God is one of the most challenging aspects Christians face as they mature in Christ. Many want to hear God's voice so that they can make the best decisions, obey God, and follow the course of life God has predetermined for them.

Often, many Christians struggle to hear the voice of God because they are unsure of how to hone their ability to hear Him. They doubt His ability to speak directly to them and they depend on others to get a "word" from God for them. Although God has given us trusted leaders to lead us, guide us, and provide us with wise counsel through words that they have received from God for us, we can build upon those words by hearing from God ourselves. This is the walk of a maturing believer, going from dependence upon "the sincere milk of the Word of God" to readiness for the "meat" of His Word.

Hearing in His Will

Many Christians believe that if they could only hear God, it would prevent them from making costly mistakes and taking unnecessary risks. This is why it's important to determine the three Ws of God:

His Word, His will, and His way.[38] This is the process of determining the Word of God on a matter, His specific will about it, and His way to fulfill it.

While God provides us with information about His Word, will, and way, God never gives us a life to live that makes Him unnecessary. Therefore, no matter how much you may want to avoid all risks, some risks are inevitable and required in a life of faith. This does not mean that God doesn't provide a course of direction for your life, but sometimes He waits for you to take the risk, to make the jump, and walk the first step in faith before He responds to you.

However, God is not just a responsive God. He often speaks to us before we have to make critical decisions and He expects us to obey him. One of the biggest questions concerning our identities is, how do you walk in your identity without knowing what the Father is specifically saying to you? How do you obey the voice of God and His "present truth" (i.e., what He is saying right now, in present time, not *just* what is written in the Word that has already occurred or is directed at the full body of Christ) if you cannot hear Him? How do we lean into His voice for clarity, direction, and wisdom for our everyday lives?

First, we should know that we serve a God who not only hears us but has the ability to speak to us. If we know this, here are a few questions that we should ask ourselves:

- ❖ Do I have the faith to believe that God is speaking and wants to speak to me?
- ❖ Do I believe that God speaks?
- ❖ If so, how often do I hear God speak?
- ❖ How do I know that it is God is speaking to me and not the enemy?
- ❖ Am I hearing the voice of God or my own thoughts?
- ❖ Is He not speaking, or have I not learned how to listen?
- ❖ How do I know or learn the voice of God?

---

[38] Bill Hamon, *Prophets and Personal Prophecy: God's Prophetic Voice Today* (Shippensburg, PA: Destiny Image, 1987).

- ❖ What does God's voice sound like?
- ❖ What can I do to hear God's voice more clearly and more often?
- ❖ How do I build a relationship with God that prompts Him to want to speak to me?
- ❖ How do I seek Him intently to hear what He is saying?

Study to Hear

Since God sounds like His Word, in order to hear Him speak, you must become a student of His written Word. God provides revelation from His written Word, which is called *logos*. He also speaks words that are called *rhema*, which is the Greek word for "utterance." These utterances are the inspired revelation that God gives to His people for direction, clarity, instruction, counsel, and wisdom.

One thing to remember is that the *logos*, God's written Word, is God speaking to the entire body of Christ as a whole. These are the big-picture directions that apply to our walk with Him. They outline how we should live, walk, and obey as Christians in our daily walk and in our everyday circumstances. The *rhema*, or the inspired Word of God, should always be congruent with God's written Word. God is not going to speak something to you in the form of *rhema* that goes against His written Word. For example, God is not going to speak a "word" to you to steal someone's car because they left the keys in the car and you don't have a car or a ride. This is not a blessing! I know this example is silly, but you may be amazed at what people have said that God has told them. God would never instruct anyone to steal.

Because every voice you hear does not come from God, it is important to have a foundation of God's written Word to avoid deception. It is equally important to be acquainted with what God's "truth" is and be careful not to rely on your own interpretation of what His written Word states. You should never use the Word of God to support your desires but you should seek his Word and "test every desire and thought against it" before you move to make any decisions. More detailed information about this process can be found in Dr. Bill Hamon's book *Prophets and Personal Prophecy: God's Prophetic Voice Today*.

Faith Comes by Hearing

Our communication relationship with God is built by faith because we cannot have any type of connection with Him outside of faith. So we must believe that God wants to speak to us and that He wants to share His mind with us. In fact, God has more ways to communicate to us than we have to truly hear Him.

Romans 10:17 says, "So then faith cometh by hearing, and hearing by the Word of God" (KJV). We must understand His written Word and hear His inspired word by faith. Hebrews 11:6 reminds us that "it is impossible to please God without faith. Anyone who wants to come to him must believe that God exists and that he rewards those who sincerely seek him" (NLT). When we seek God with our whole hearts, not with our feelings, or emotions, He is ready and quick to speak to us.

God speaks to our inner man, which is our spiritual selves. Although this list is not all-encompassing, He may speak audibly or through our conscious thoughts, dreams, visions, prophecy, or even through supernatural encounters. When God speaks to us, we may receive a spiritual impression from Him that is undeniable. It is important that we hold on to these impressions and apply our faith to them; if we do not, the enemy will try to convince us that we have not heard from God.

Listening Closely

When you are first learning to hear God's voice, it may *sound* like the strongest authority figure in your life, such as your pastor, mother, or father. You may hear their voice when it is God speaking to your conscious mind. However, as you mature, this sound may change. A large part of hearing God is connected to your level of faith and how disciplined you are to listen.

God responds to faith. If you want to hear God more, you are going to have to increase your faith. Not only does your faith has to increase to a level where you are able to believe that God can and will speak to you daily but you must learn to listen daily and wait intently to hear Him. Listening requires you to silence your own thoughts and prayers and prevent yourself from speaking. This is not the time to speak and pour out your heart but a time to simply listen by faith and record what you hear God is saying to you.

This requires devotion and spending time with Him. I'm not referring to reading a devotional someone else wrote or your favorite commentary. I'm talking about spending time reading through the Bible for context, content, history, information, and revelation. I'm suggesting that you take notes and learn the mind and thought processes of God. Then ask your questions to God. We call these types of requests supplications because they are targeted petitions that we make to God, who is our King.

Sometimes if you do not ask the "right" questions, you will not get the answer you are looking for. We have countless examples of individuals asking Jesus questions, only to witness Him responding to things they should have asked. Other times we watch as He gives them answers to questions they did not ask. This is because if we ask questions that do not align with what God wants to reveal, we may be asking amiss.

Testing What You Have Heard

Some ways to identify when God is speaking to you on a matter is to determine the level of spiritual peace you have, identify any "checks" in your spirit, seek and obtain wise counsel, and seek confirmation. Spiritual peace according to Psalms 34:4 is a level of tranquility that guards your heart and mind through Christ. It is the assurance that the decisions you are making do not bring fear, anxiety, worry, or self-reliance. You will have a peace that rules in your spirit and governs every decision. A rule of thumb is that if you do not have the "spiritual peace" on a situation, do not act upon it, until you seek God for more clarity.

Sometimes, time constraints limit our ability to wait for spiritual peace. This is the time to seek wise counsel. Although Jesus is our greatest counselor, in Proverbs 11:14 we are reminded, "Where no counsel is, the people fall: but in the multitude of counsellors there is safety." Wise counsel may be necessary before making some decisions. Sometimes, the Holy Spirit will give you a "check" to warn you about something. This is a type of warning that challenges you to pause before deciding. It's important to not ignore these sorts of promptings because God could be working to reveal more important information to prevent you from falling into a blunder. Whenever you feel a need to pause, stop and seek God more intently.

Lastly, God often provides spiritual confirmation concerning His plans for you. There are several scriptures that speak about the Word of God being confirmed through the "word" or the "mouth" of two or three witnesses: "This is the third time I am coming to you. In the mouth of two or three witnesses shall every word be established" (Second Corinthians 13:1 KJV). However, Romans 8:16 states that the Holy Spirit should "bear witness" or align with the Spirit of God that dwells within our inner man.

Not only does the Holy Spirit within us confirm that we are the sons and daughters of God, it also confirms if something is "Spirit-led" or not. If something doesn't resonate with the character and integrity of God, it is most likely not Spirit-led. Remember, 2 Peter 1:3 reminds us that God, through His divine power, has given us everything we need that pertains to our life and to the godliness that He has established for us to live by. All confirmations we receive should be congruent with His divine power and the Holy Spirit.

Stop and Reflect

God is speaking… It's time to hear Him more…

1. Are you consistently hearing the voice of God? If not, why?
2. Have you researched God's will in an area in which you desire to hear Him more deeply and more intently?
3. If you consistently hear the voice of God, do you test everything you have heard by His written Word?
4. When you feel that God has spoken to you about something, where do you look for confirmation? Have you sought confirmation outside of Word of God or His will?

5. What sorts of things have you used to decide you have received confirmation other than Word of God? For example, are you using the result of a situation for confirmation, or have you identified that the result is the work of the enemy and not God?

6. How do you know if something has been confirmed? How do you know if you have received false confirmation?

7. How can you learn to seek confirmation by God and not by observation, a result of something, or by your opinion?

Chapter 10

Who Are You *Really?*

In His Likeness: Your Spiritual Genetics

In Genesis chapter 1, Moses explains to us that in the beginning, God created the heavens, the earth, and much more. These scriptures go on to explain everything God created and how God viewed His creation. Learning to live in your truest, most authentic self requires that you understand who *you* really are. This is not just an idea that encompasses your strengths, personality, desires, habits, or ideals. Rather, it is understanding that you are created in the image and likeness of God.

If we explore biblical genealogy, we will discover that although everyone is God's creation, not everyone is a son of God.[39] Let's explore this concept further. If I have the DNA of both my mother and my father, I will have characteristics that reflect them both. I may share my mother's eye shape while sharing my father's thick eyebrows. I may share my father's height and share my mother's lip shape. All of the DNA that makes me who I am is a direct result of my genes inherited from my parents.

Even if I go further back, I will find DNA that resembles my grandparents and ancestors. Genesis 5:3 states, "And Adam lived a hundred and thirty years, and begat a son in his own likeness, and after

---

[39] R. Watson Jr., "Foundations Class, Part 4: Faith" (July 1, 2019).

his image; and called his name Seth." Seth is Adam's son because he was created and made in his father's likeness and in his image, meaning that he carried both his human spirit and his genetic makeup. Luke 3:38 explains to us the genealogy of Adam and identifies that he was "the son of God." First John 5:1 tells us that "Whosoever believeth that Jesus is the Christ is born of God: and every one that loveth him that begat, loveth him also that is begotten of him." What these three scriptures explain to us is that in order to be a "son" of someone, your birth must have come from them. Only those who believe that Jesus is the Christ is born of God. So although we are all God's creation, only those who are born again can claim to be God's sons and daughters.

Furthermore, 1 John 1:2 explains to us that if we claim to be sons of God, we will carry the DNA of love, and that love will be scientifically proven by our willingness to keep and obey God's commandments. This is not referring to the Ten Commandments but every word and expectation God has for all His sons and daughters; these are found in His written Word.

First John 1:4 says that whatever is born of God conquerors the world, meaning the systems, ideologies, policies, and wisdom that operates on earth. All of our victories are achieved through the faith that is given to us by a product of our belief. This conquering power that operates through our faith brings the "world to its knees." Therefore, faith conquers the world and its systems. Faith operates outside of our human logic, nature, and humanistic characteristics. Faith operates by its own system of rules created by God. Thus, since we believe that Jesus is the Son of God, as a byproduct of our belief in Him we conquer the world.

As I mentioned in the beginning of this chapter, God is the ultimate Creator. He is the Creator of all things, including personalities, dance, music, ethnicities, gifts, talents, and almost anything you can imagine. It is He who creates. I must mention, however, that Satan loves to pervert the things that God has created to make them morph into things that God never intended. This is why we see perversion in dance, music, art, and other cultural aspects of life. But just because Satan has perverted some things in creation does not mean that God did not have beautiful, pure intentions for everything that He created. Satan is a mocker, an imitator, and the father of lies. Everything that he orchestrates is from his kingdom.

The reason why this is important to understand is that if you are made in God's image and in His likeness, your life should manifest His creative abilities and powers. I once spoke to an individual who was a massive planner. They really didn't want to do anything in their life without having a plan. They felt that this was a personality flaw that got in the way of their relationship with God. I explained to them that because they are born of God, and He is their Creator, the fact that this person was a master planner was a direct reflection of God's identity in them. You see, God is the biggest planner in all the earth. He uniquely planned the earth, the weeks, months, sun, moon, stars, human beings, and much more. So when we manifest creativity or express our personalities, they are and should be a direct reflection of the One who created us. It should be evident that we are our Father's children.

Sons and Daughters

There are three main tenets to salvation: justification, sanctification, and glorification. It is by reason of our belief in Christ that we access salvation. This is what provides us the opportunity to be reborn spiritually in order to be made in the likeness and image of God. When Adam sinned in the garden, his sin caused a spiritual death, and this death separated Adam from the glory of God. When we decide to be born again, we are committing to allow our old spirit and old nature to die so that our new godly spirit may be resurrected in Christ.

One way this is demonstrated is through baptism by water. Adam's sin brought spiritual death to every human, but through Jesus's death and resurrection, He brought life to every human who believes in Him. First Corinthians 15:21 says, "So you see, just as death came into the world through a man, now the resurrection from the dead has begun through another man" (NLT). When we are baptized by water, we are willingly giving up our liberty to live for ourselves and instead live for Jesus, who died for our sins (Second

Corinthians 5:14–15). The process of justification, sanctification, and glorification is what makes us sons and daughters of God.

Justification is the separation from the penalty of sin. Sanctification is the separation from the power of sin. Glorification is the separation from the presence of sin.[40] All of these tenets operate in three tenses: past, present, and future. Romans 8:30 says, "Moreover whom he did predestinate, them he also called: and whom he called, them he also justified: and whom he justified, them he also glorified" (KJV).

Justification operates in the past tense because it was what was done for you by reason of your belief. Romans 5:1–2 says, "Therefore being justified by faith, we have peace with God through our Lord Jesus Christ: By whom also we have access by faith into this grace wherein we stand and rejoice in hope of the glory of God." Because you have chosen to be born again, you are justified. Justification is what makes you God-conscious.

What's important to remember about justification is that you cannot earn it, you cannot work for it, and you cannot prove that you are worthy of it. You simply access justification by faith. This means that there is nothing you can do to earn God's love, acceptance, and approval. He willingly and freely gives it to you through justification.

Sanctification functions in the present tense because it is the work of God's Spirit inside of you on a daily basis. The Greek word for sanctification is *hagiazó* (hag-ee-ad'-zo); it literally means "to make holy, consecrate, to set apart as holy, to regard as special (sacred); to set apart."[41] Through God's spirit, sanctification is the power that you have been given by the Spirit of God to overcome sin daily. It is an ongoing process that doesn't end until you die. It is the process of choosing regularly to not walk in sin or allow sin to be your master. Romans 6:6 says, "Knowing this, that our old man is crucified with him, that the body of sin might be destroyed, that henceforth we should not serve sin" (KJV).

---

[40] O. Guobadia, "Prophets," presented online via Facebook (accessed live January 19, 2018).

[41] *Bible Hub: Strong's Greek Concordance Online*, s.v. "hagiazó" (https://biblehub.com/greek/37.htm).

Glorification is the process of obtaining an incorruptible body where no more sin will be in existence. It is the future tense of what every born-again believer will walk into. Philippians 3:21 says, "Who shall change our vile body, that it may be fashioned like unto his glorious body, according to the working whereby he is able even to subdue all things unto himself" (KJV). The purpose of a glorified body is so that we can live and reign with God in the future.

Purpose

One Greek word for sin is *hamartia* (ham-ar-tee'-ah), and it means to "miss the mark, to fail, and to forfeit."[42] Romans 3:23 says, "For all have sinned, and come short of the glory of God." If the definition of sin is to miss the mark, then what is the mark that is missed? Missing the mark or sinning is falling short of the glory of God. Thus, "sin" is act of missing the mark and the target of carrying God's glory.

Second Thessalonians 2:13–14 explains to us that from the beginning, God intended for us, through salvation, to access the gospel, and thereby obtain or "carry" the glory of God. It is through this process that we become "glory carriers" and we find our entire purpose on earth.

The main point of salvation and the gospel is not for us to simply be able to go to heaven but to reobtain our original purpose, which is carrying and releasing God's glory. Once we are born again, God is able to put His glory back within us. The Greek word for glory is *doxa*[43] (dox'-ah). This parallels with the Old Testament word *kabo*, which means "to be heavy." Both of these words express God's infinite, intrinsic worth, substance, and essence). Glory is a truly divine essence expressed as heavenly worth and quality. Therefore, the purpose of salvation is to make mankind everything that God *originally* intended. This answers the question of why we are born

---

[42] *Bible Hub: Strong's Greek Concordance Online*, s.v. "hamartia" (https://biblehub.com/greek/266.htm).

[43] *Bible Hub: Strong's Greek Concordance Online*, s.v. "doxa" (retrieved July 23, 2020, from https://biblehub.com/str/greek/1391.htm).

and why we exist, leading us to our ultimate purpose in life, which is to demonstrate God's glory.

Not only does our relationship with God pave the way for us to demonstrate God's glory, it also gives us a "right of entry" into eternal life. Here we should draw the distinction between eternal life and everlasting life. Eternal life is not just life after death. It's experiencing life with God now. John 17:1–3 says,

> These words spake Jesus, and lifted up his eyes to heaven, and said, Father, the hour is come; glorify thy Son, that thy Son also may glorify thee: As thou hast given him power over all flesh, that he should give eternal life to as many as thou hast given him. And **this is life eternal, that they might know thee the only true God, and Jesus Christ, whom thou hast sent**. This lets us know that eternal life is "that we may know him, the only true God, and Jesus Christ who was sent. (KJV, emphasis mine)

Eternal means "without beginning or end, always existing, lasting forever."[44] Since God is a spirit, He is eternal. He has no beginning and no end. When we access eternal life, we are entering into a spiritual relationship with God that exists outside of time as we know it. We are coming into the knowledge of learning who God is. On the other hand, everlasting life refers to life that lasts for a very long time or for an indefinitely long time. Everlasting life is speaking of a type of life that did not always exist but that, through God, is given to those who are believers.

---

[44] Nimisha Kaushik, "Difference Between Eternal and Everlasting," *Difference Between.net* (May 7, 2011, retrieved July 23, 2020, from http://www.differencebetween.net/language/difference-between-eternal-and-everlasting/).

Calling/Assignment

You may be thinking at this point, *I already know that I am a son or daughter of Christ, but what is my calling? What have I been put on this earth to do?* Don't worry, I get it. This is a question that many people have spent a lifetime trying to better understand. The reason I started with a discussion of your purpose and identity in the Father is because every assignment that you ever have should flow from your identity in the Father. If you are seeking to learn your calling so that you feel validated, affirmed, or accepted; or so that you can prove wrong everyone who counted you out; or so you can feel self-worth, self-esteem, or self-importance; you are not ready to walk in your ultimate calling. It is likely that whatever your ultimate calling or purpose is on earth will remain obscure until you learn to live completely as a son or daughter of God.

What this means is that until you understand in the depths of your heart that the only affirmation, validation, and acceptance that you need and should crave comes from a relationship with the Father, you will likely not understand your purpose fully. The more you work on building this relationship, the more you will understand how your individual gifts will be used to help you manifest your calling.

More than anything, you should understand that you are a son or daughter of God. If you are lacking in self-esteem, validation, or affirmation, everything you do in your life will be motivated by fulfilling these deep holes. You must first understand that you are uniquely designed, a person of purpose, and a person of worth, prior to you ever doing anything.

Remember that God said to Jesus that "he was his beloved son in whom he was well pleased" (Mark 1:11) prior to Jesus performing any miracles or doing anything to earn God's contentment. It was simply by reason of His birth that God had fully accepted Him. Many people spend a lot of time trying to prove why they are worthy to be blessed, favored, or fully accepted by God. Simply by reason of being born again, God has justified and accepted you.

Again, you don't have to earn it, work for it, or do anything other than believe to qualify for God's justification. Whether you perform any "great works" or miracles does not determine your value or your worth in God's kingdom. Your value and worth is determined by simply being a son or daughter.

Once you understand your spiritual genetics completely, you can begin to seek God on what is next for your life. As you continue to deeply seek Him and walk in faith, He will begin to reveal the next steps for your calling and purpose. When you lack true identity in God, you will fulfill this void by seeking careers, friends, relationships, education, marriage, love, children, diets, food—literally anything and everything you can easily and temporarily access can become your void filler. You may find yourself in deep rejection and idolatry because you will consistently seek ways to please your own self to feel valuable and necessary.

The goal of learning who you are really is not to fulfil your voids but to come to the end of yourself and accept who God says that you are. No matter how much money you earn or what stages you may walk on one day, if you are not fulfilled by being a son or daughter in Christ, *nothing* will fulfill you completely. So ask yourself, **Who are** YOU *really?*

Stop and Reflect

Who are YOU *really?*

1. Have you been born again? If so, how effectively are you walking in your identity as a son or daughter? Are you in purpose or distracted by your own ideals of self?
2. Examine your ideas about who you are. Identify areas where you are questioning your identity, your purpose, or God's will for your life. How can you seek Him more intently to reveal your next assignment? What have you done previously that hasn't worked for you? How can you change?
3. What are some areas in which your identity puzzle needs to be reconstructed? How have you invited the Holy Spirit to rule in this area?

Conclusion

Life is a series of zigzag events. Although there are many paths and even hallways that lead to different doors, there are always several overlapping paths that can confuse, deter, distract, or even puzzle the person on the journey. Making choices about yourself, your life, and your identity is a process that is not always clear-cut, fluid, consistent, or even rewarding. However, no matter what path a person takes, they will experience both pain and purpose.

The human mind is not always prepared, disciplined, or fine-tuned enough to cope with the unexpected politics of life. Not every outcome of each decision can be anticipated, which means you will not always be in control. This is why identity must first be discovered in Christ prior to becoming completely fulfilled in life.

Lack of genuine identity steals the purpose of gifted people and leaves deep voids that suck out the powerful passions of life. When each person knows who they are, what they have to offer the world, and lives in such a way that births purpose, a new realm of freedom is obtained. However, remaining focused amid confusion requires tenacity, resilience, and zeal just as much as it requires endurance, reflection, and patience. Most of all, regaining focus and identifying who you are really meant to be requires balance and knowing who you are in Christ.

The purpose of sharing the process of discovering my identity is to help others regain focus in their life so that they can properly understand and pivot their passions in the right direction. It also shows others that through process, development, and maturity, they too can discover who they are meant to be.

About the Author

Candace Q. Powell is a lover of all things creative writing. She's a passionate poet, inspirational speaker, and creative writer who enjoys artistic expression and literature. Even more, she enjoys the chilling details, humor, and adventures that writing can bring. In writing, she offers her readers the ultimate joys of acceptance, healing, comfort, and peace. As a lover and follower of Christ, her first answer to everything is prayer and faith. It is this very combination that has brought her through life's toughest seasons.

Candace is a proud mother and wife who currently lives in North Carolina with her husband, James, and three children Audrey, Kenton, and Royce.